The Watercolor Collection of Flowers and Asian Landscapes
花與景・水彩畫集

ISBN-13 978-0997269338
ISBN-10 0997269332
First published in United States in 2018
All artworks are made by Queenie Wong
Wonger0050@yahoo.com.hk

This book contains totally 57 watercolor paintings done in 2017 and 2018.
It includes 26 flowers and 30 Asian landscapes.
Also, there are pictures show the artist's working process before the final works.
Most artworks are painted in realistic style but
the colors are dramatically applied to a quiet romantic setting.
The scenes create a calm and relaxing atmosphere to the viewers.

Book Content

Flowers 花

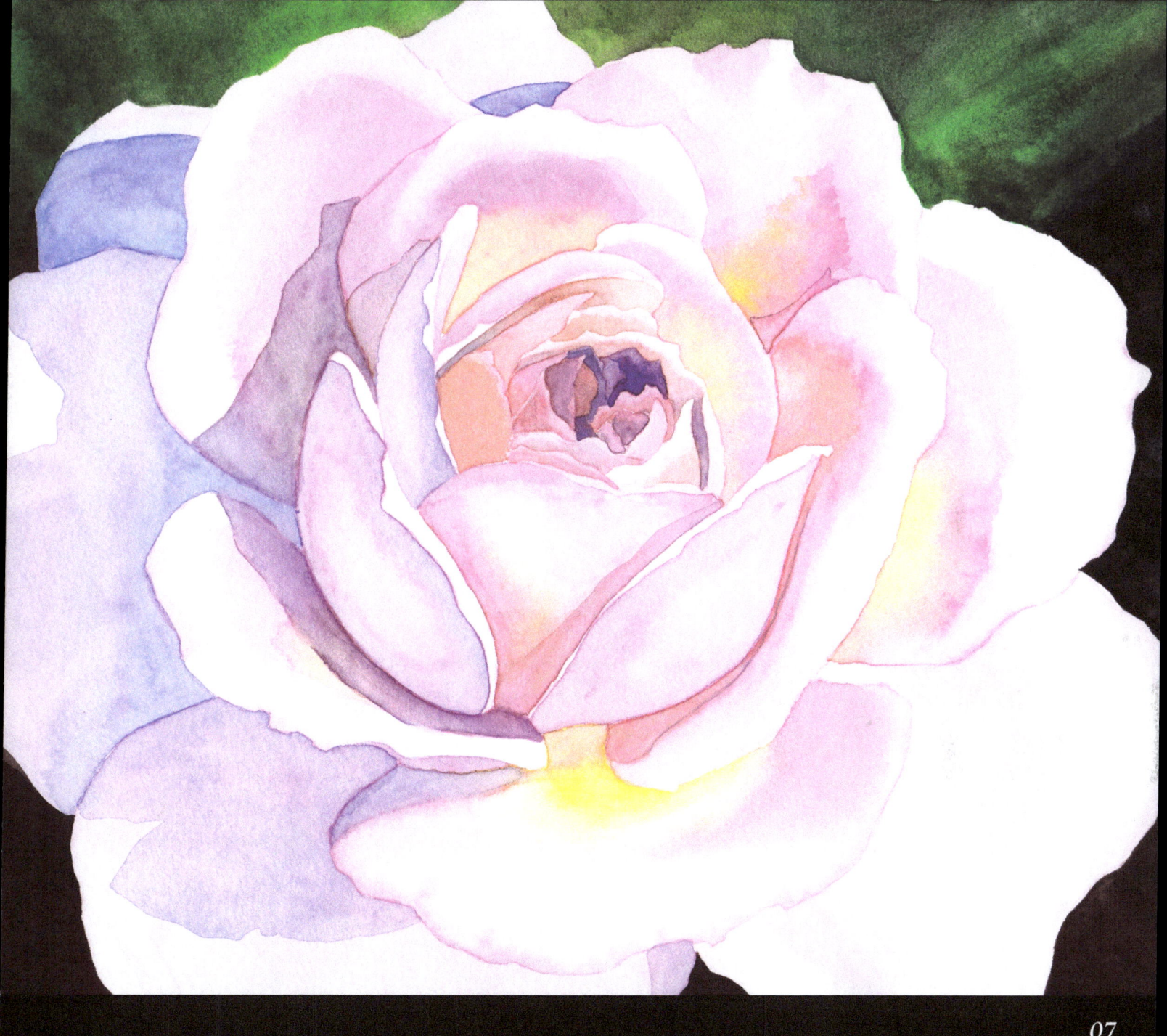

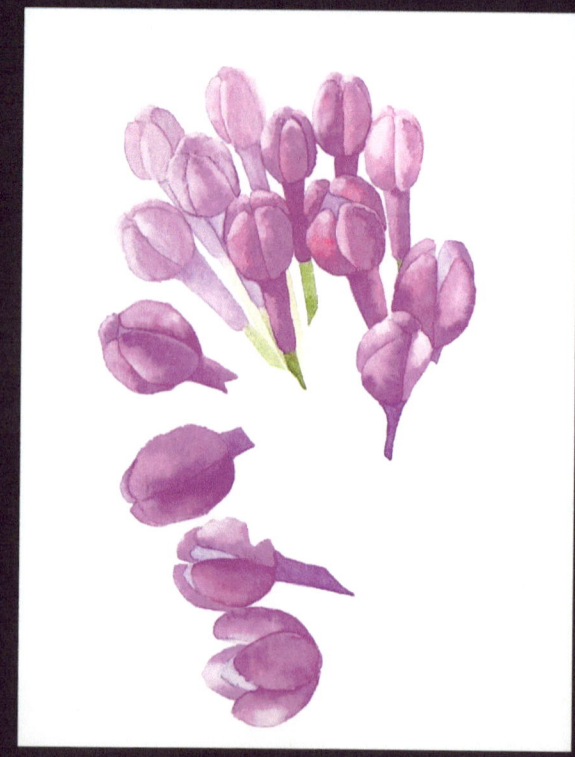

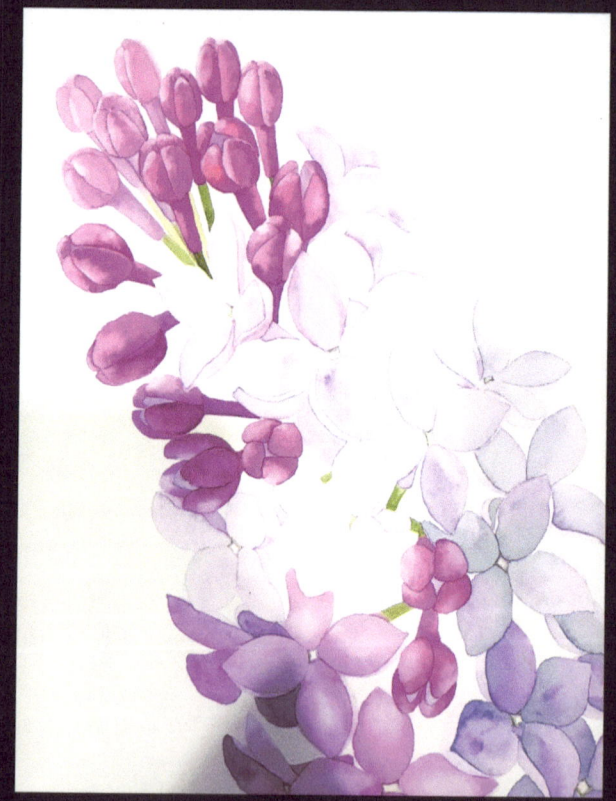

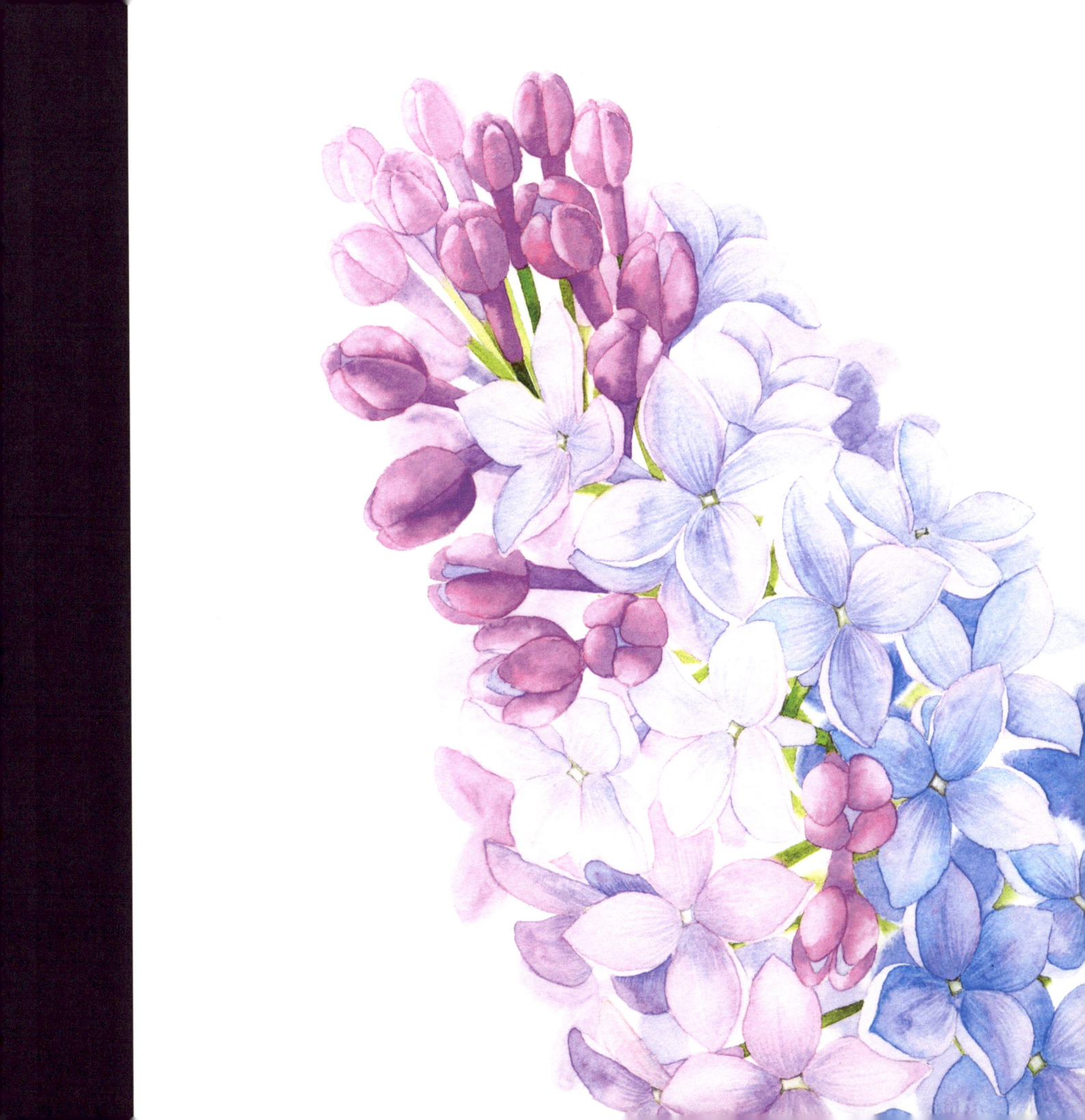

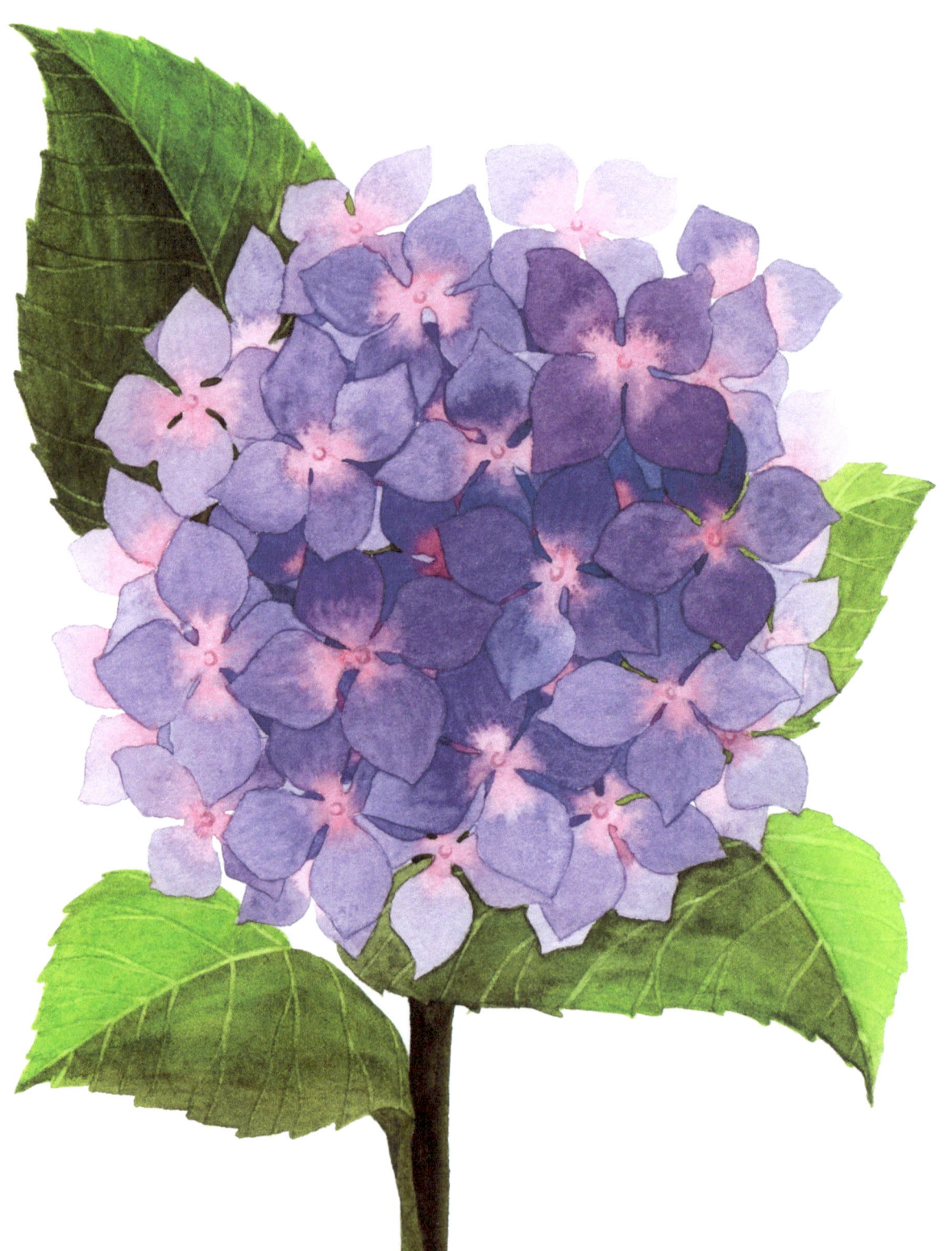

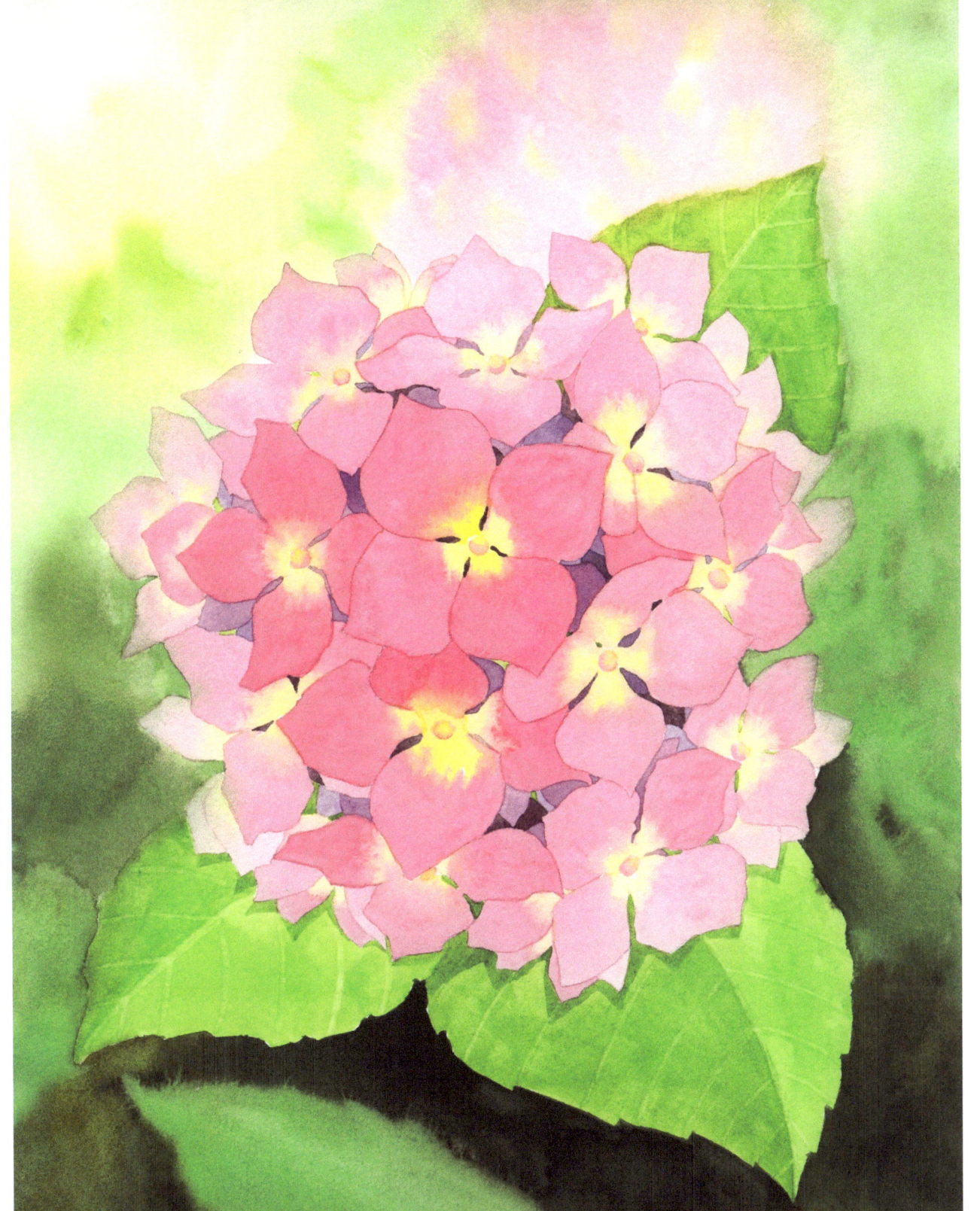

11

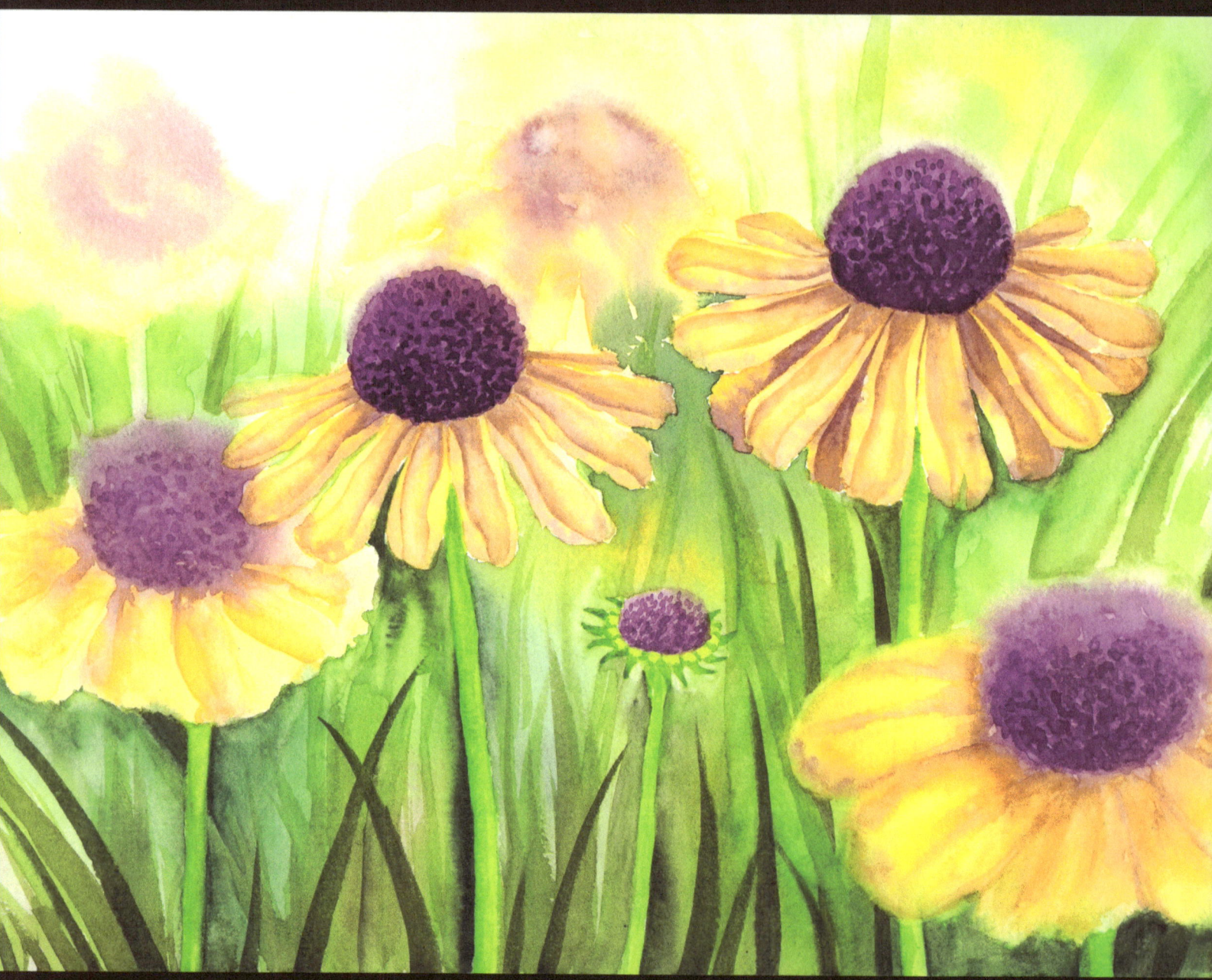

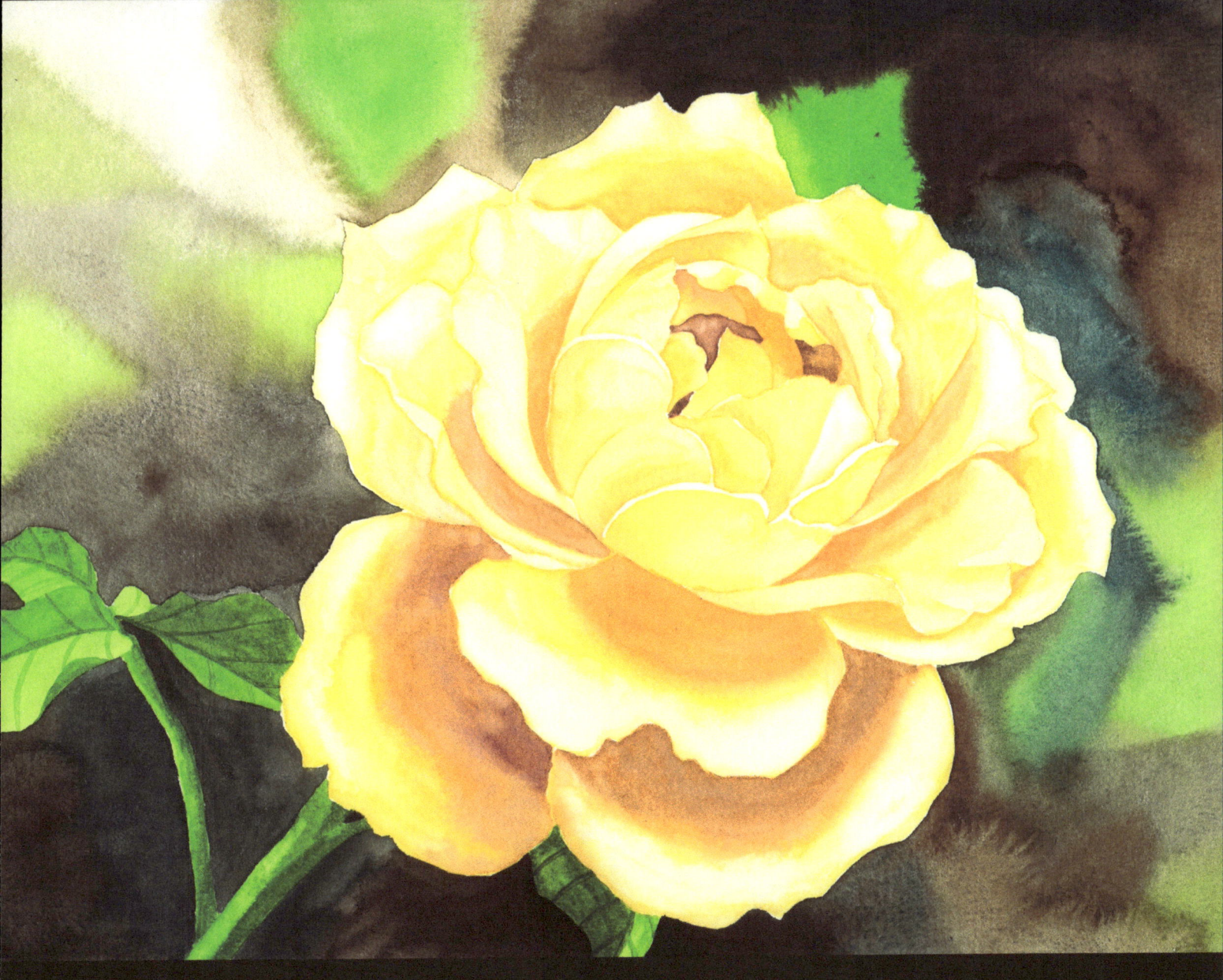

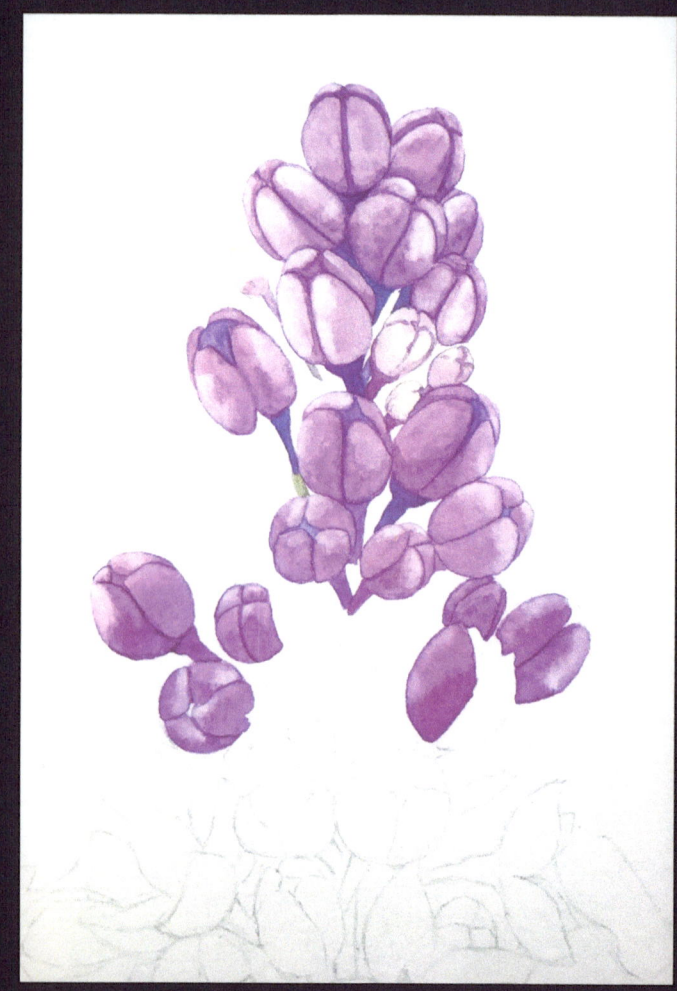

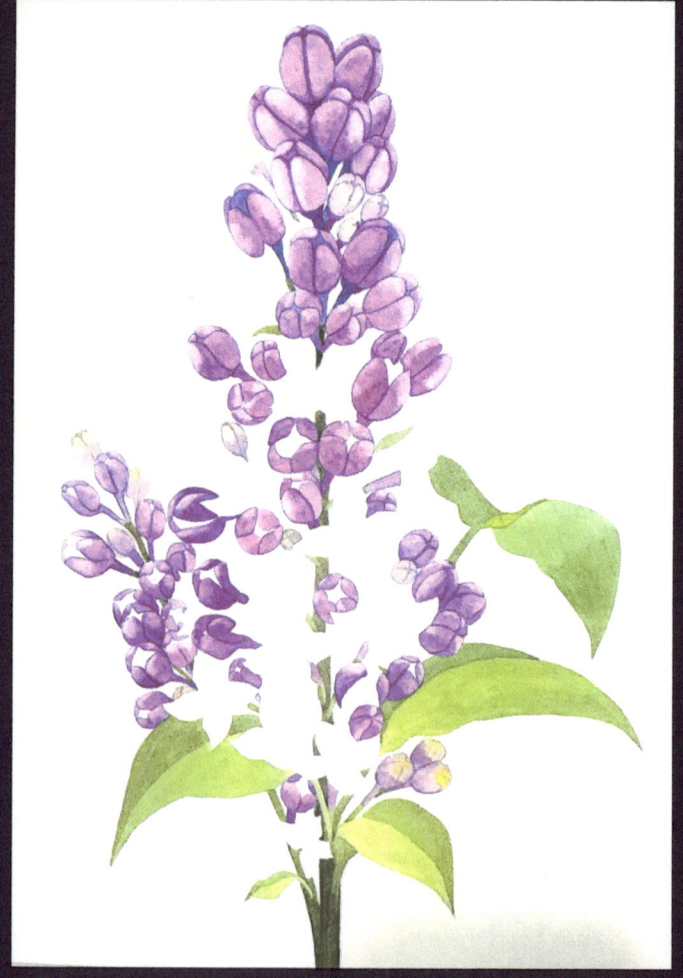

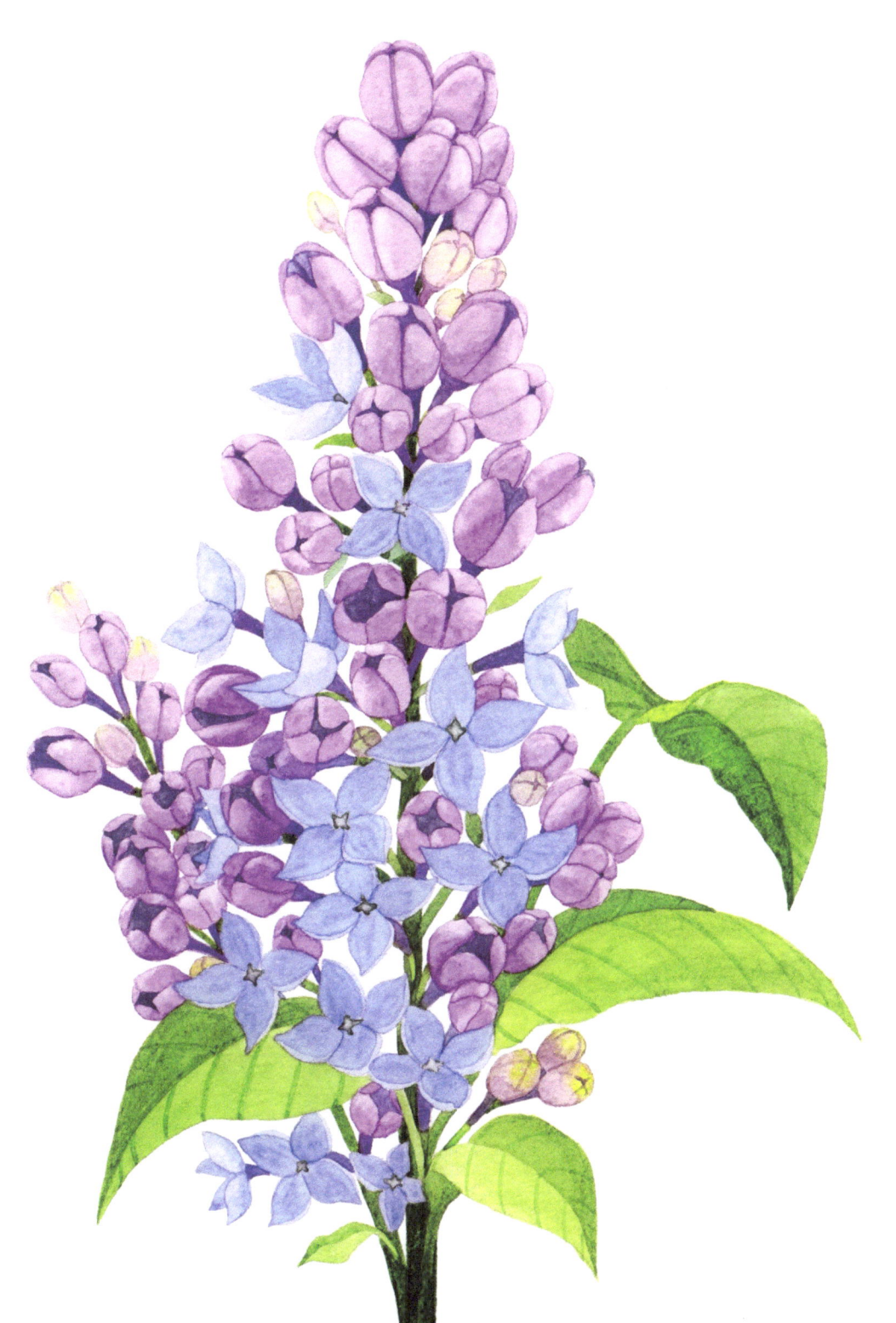

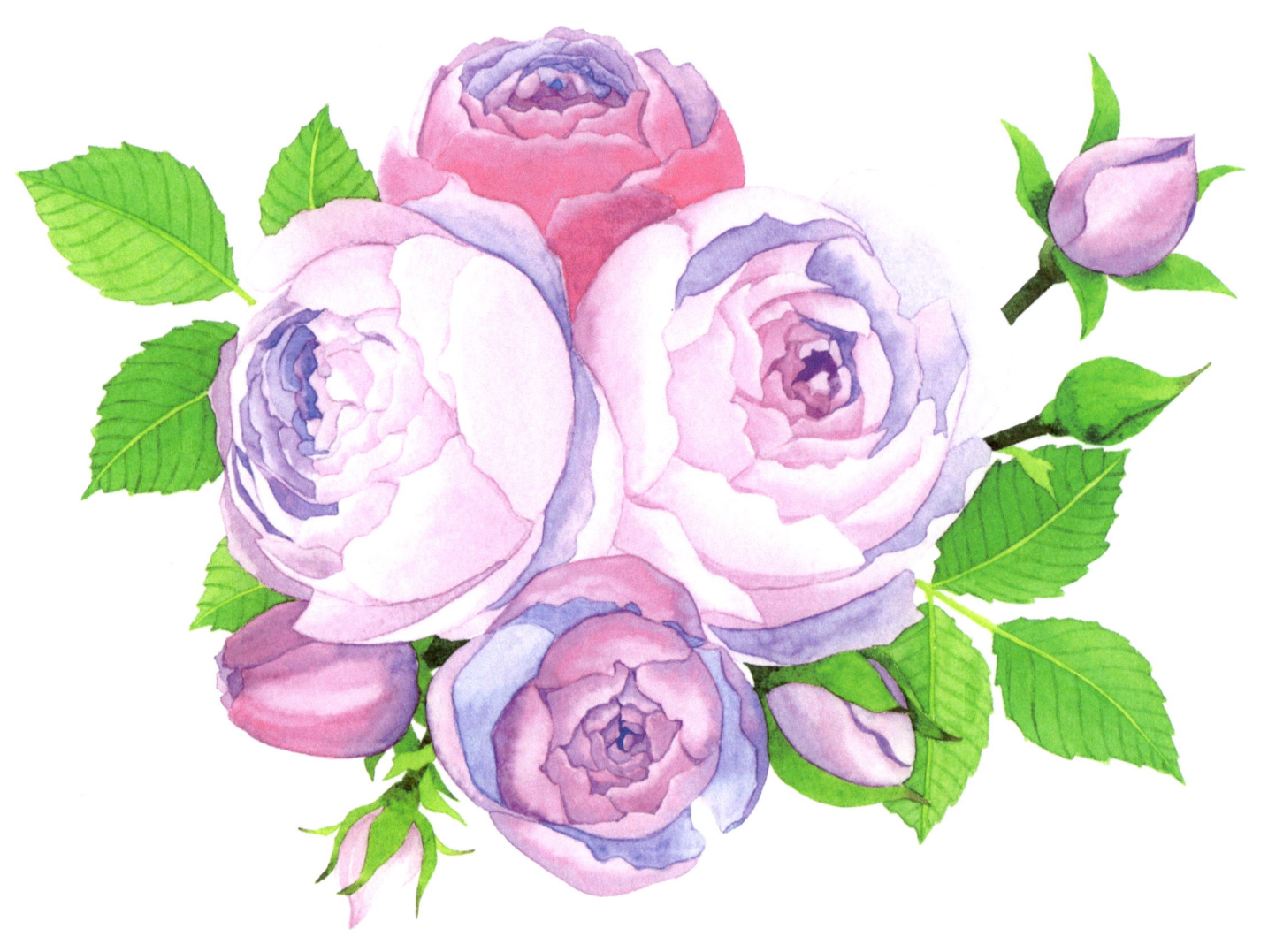

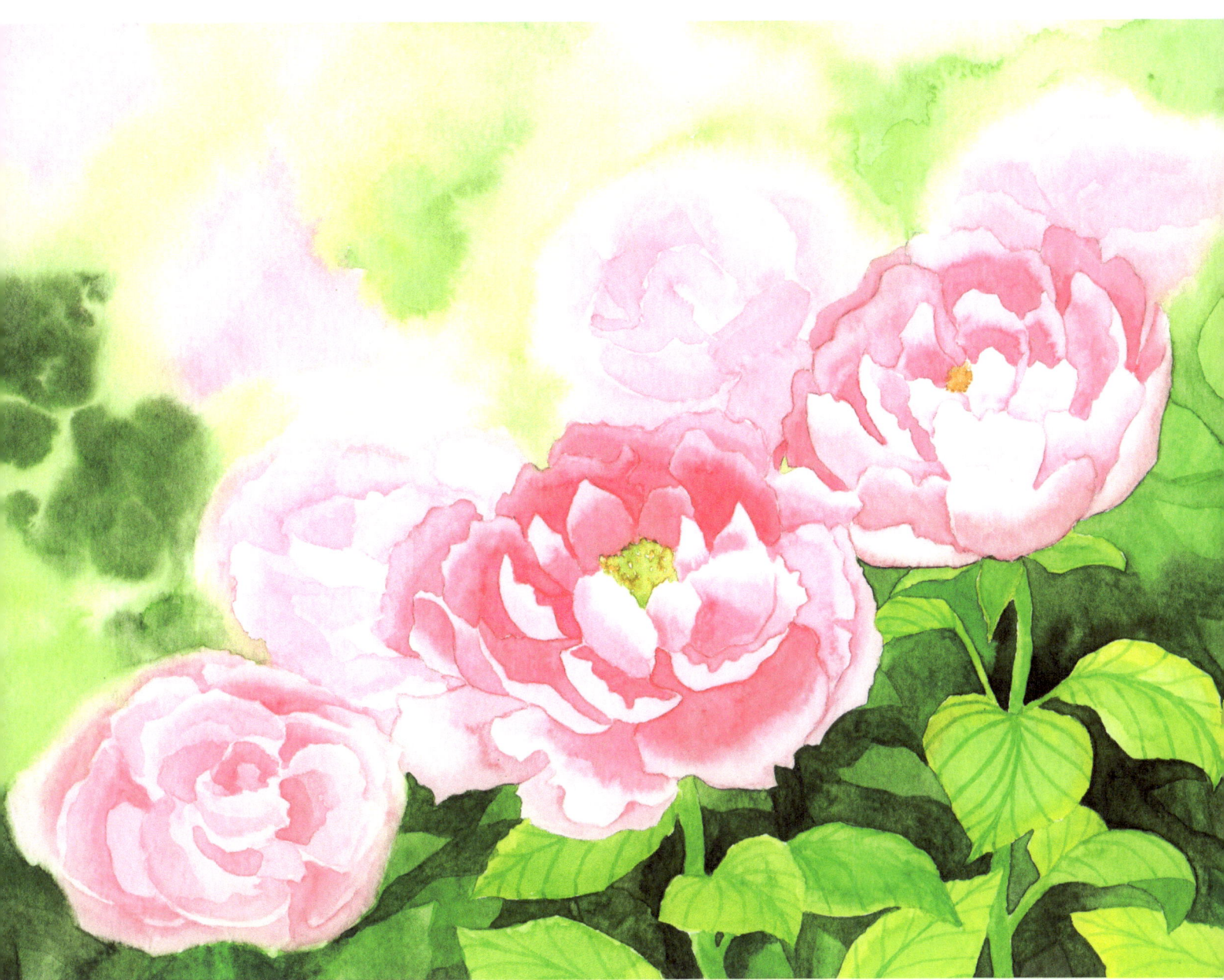

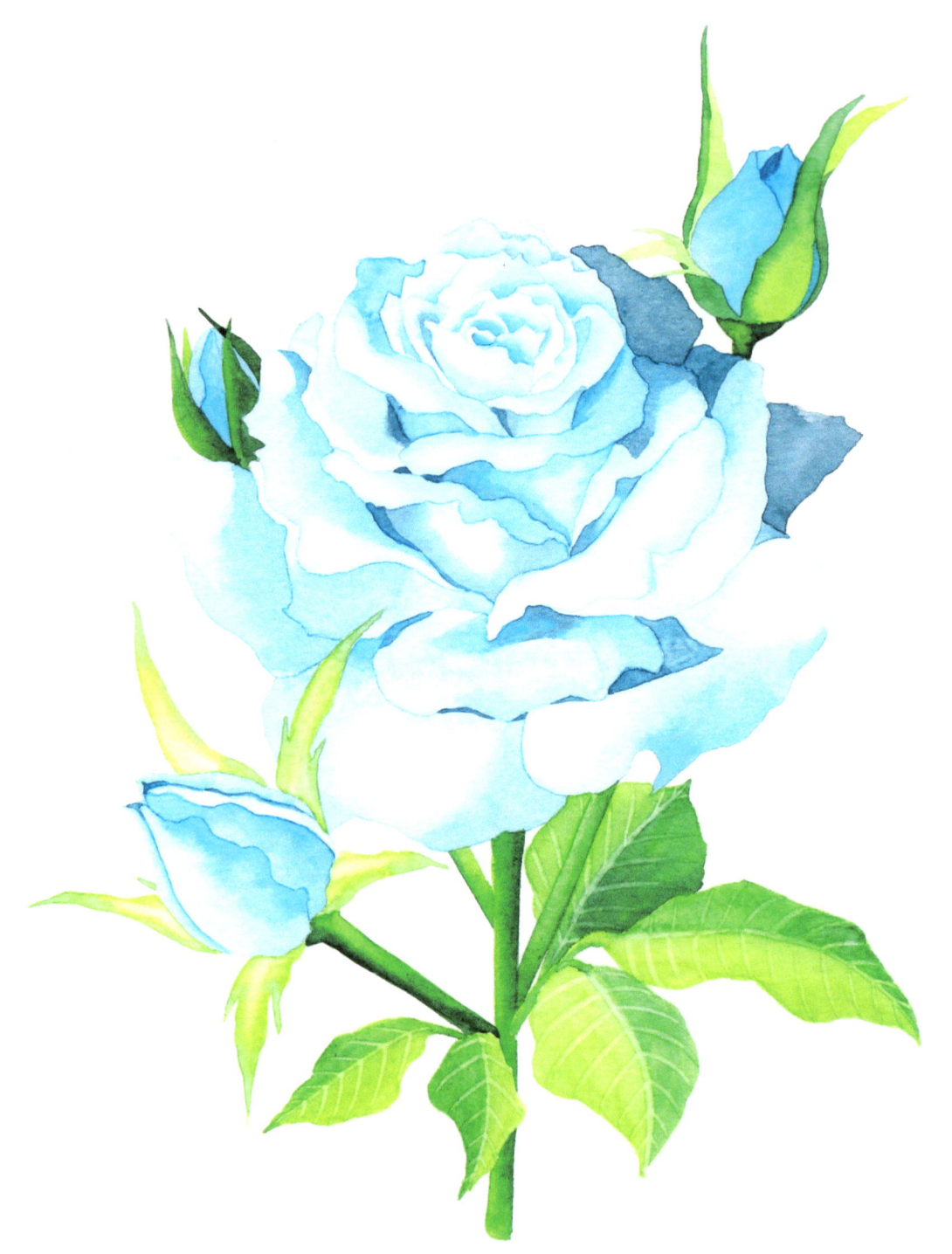

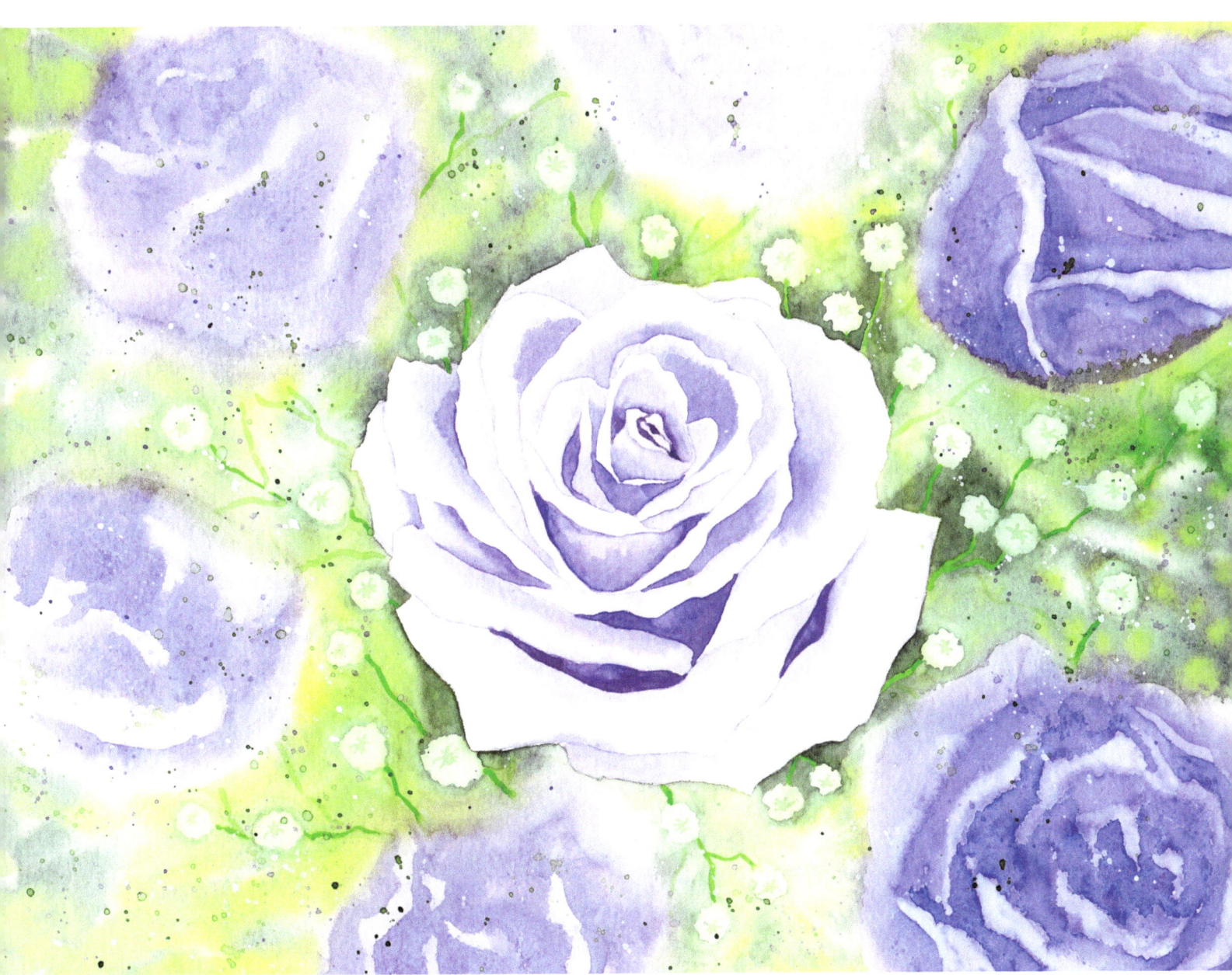

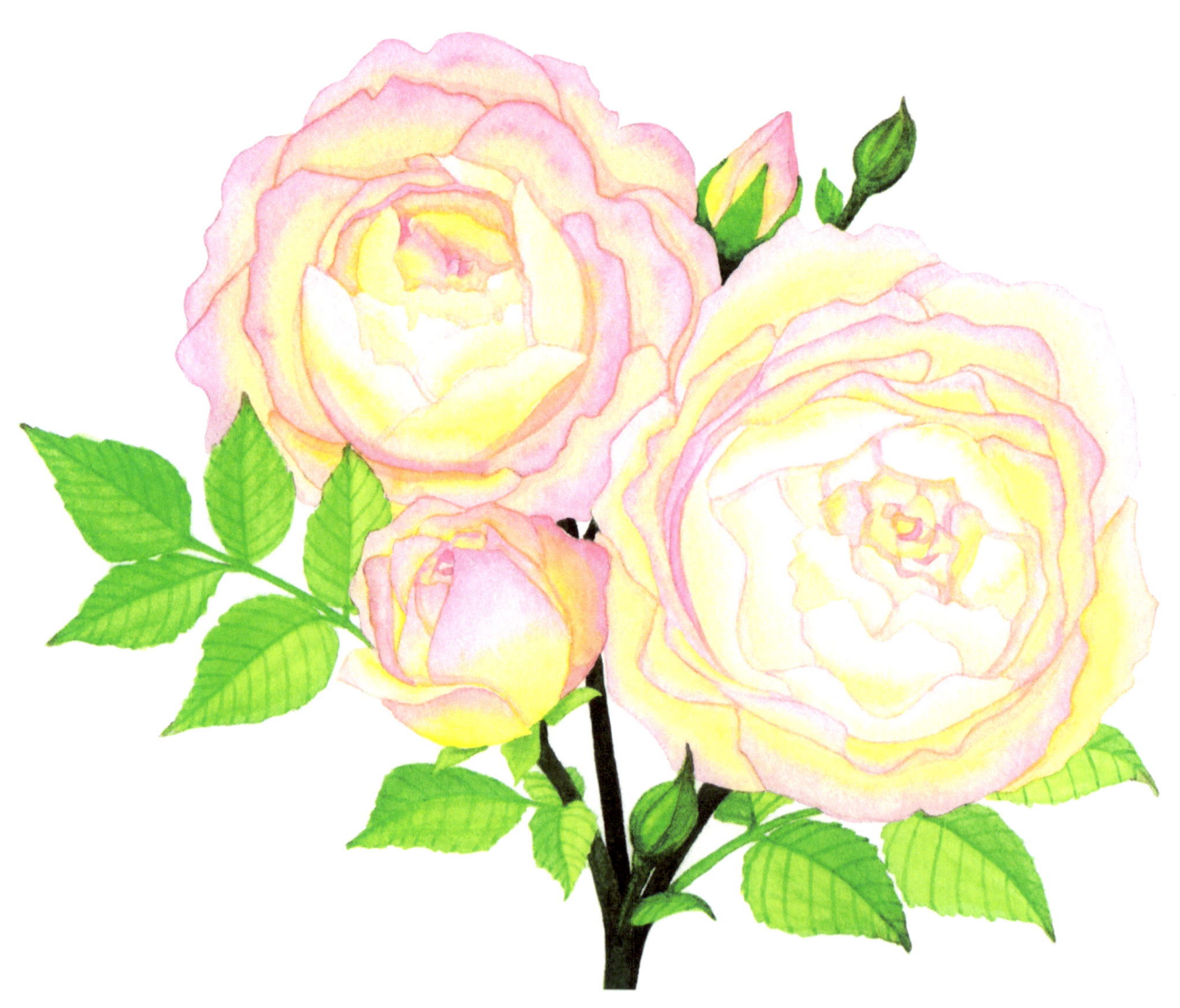

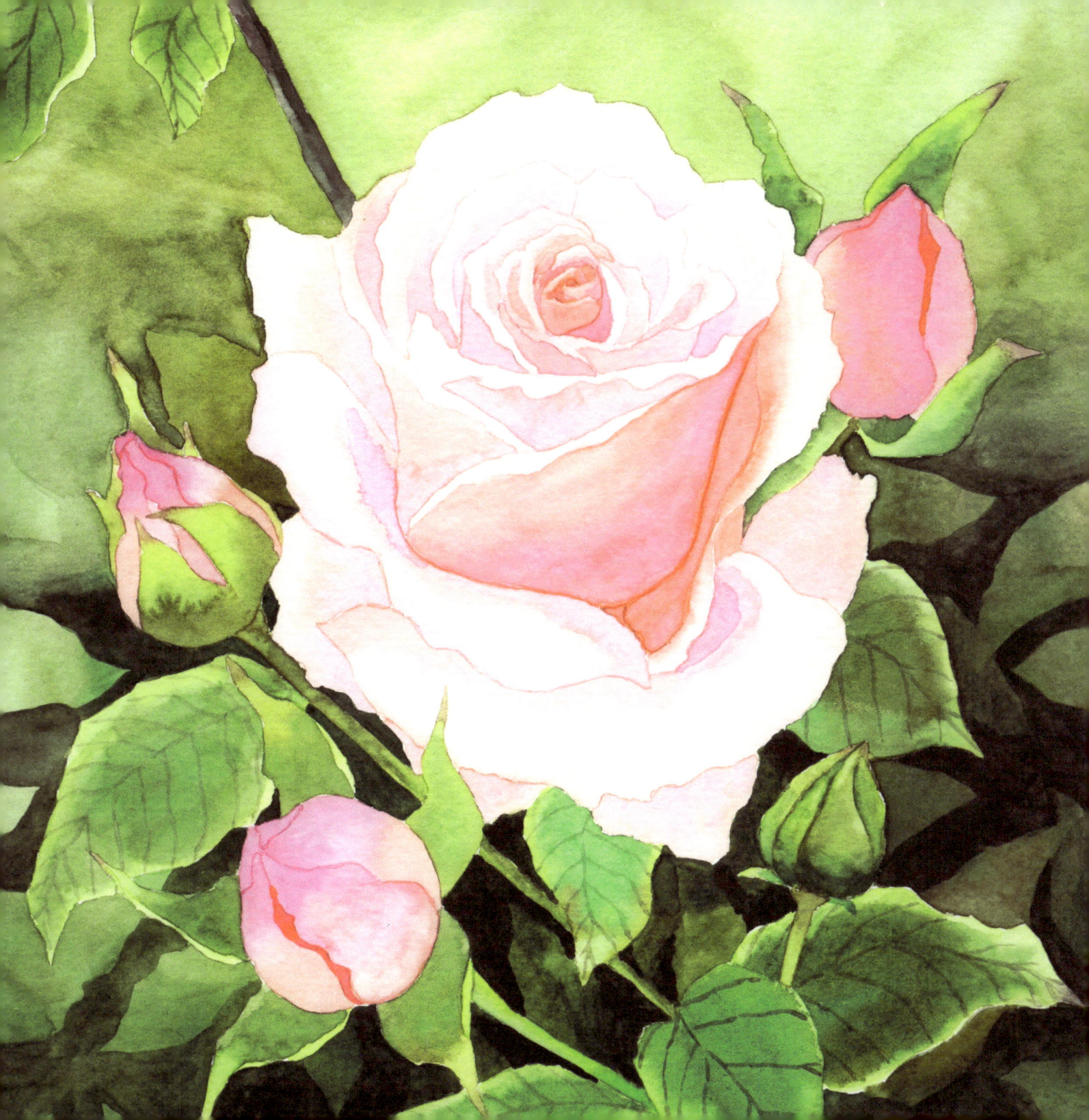

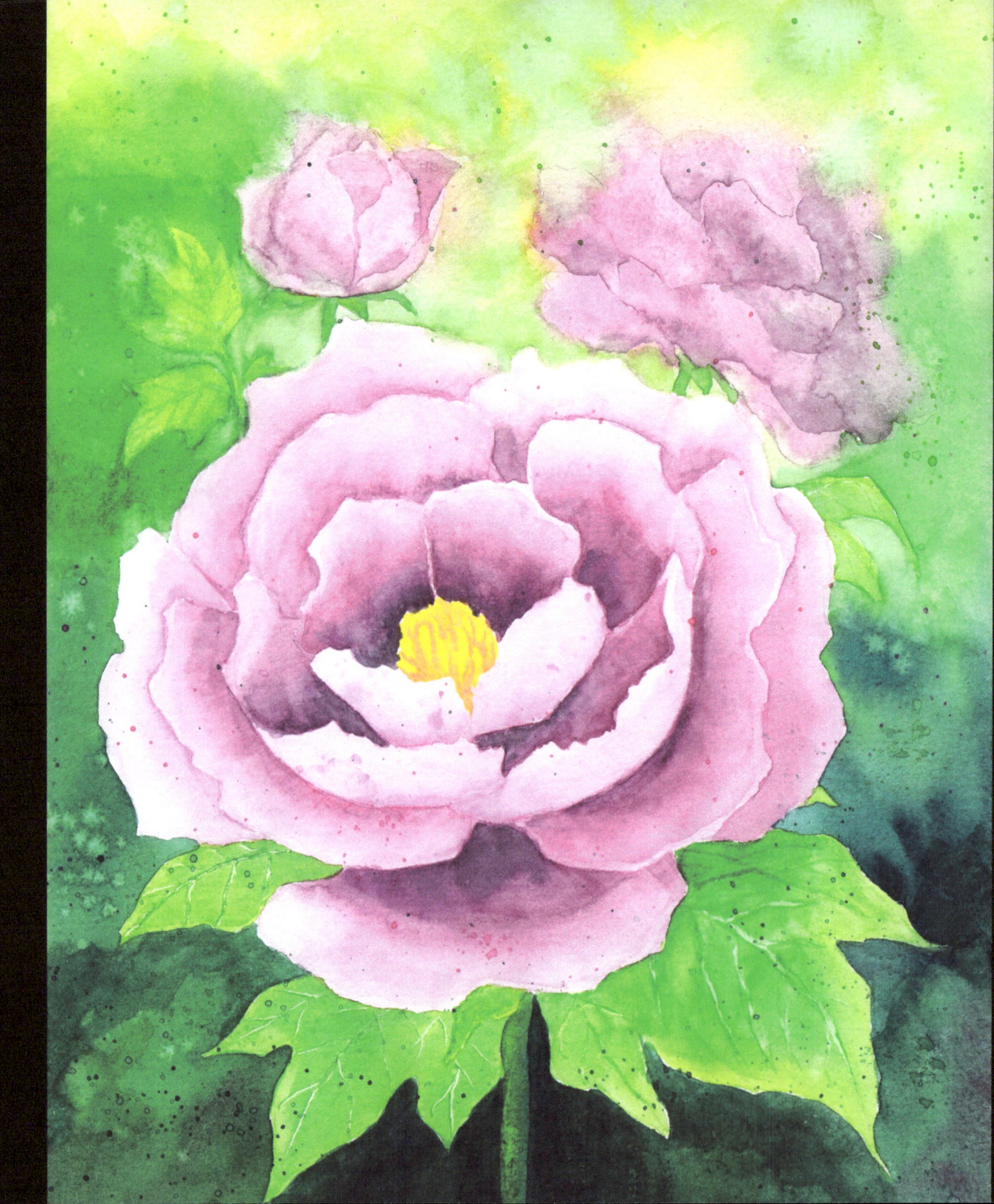

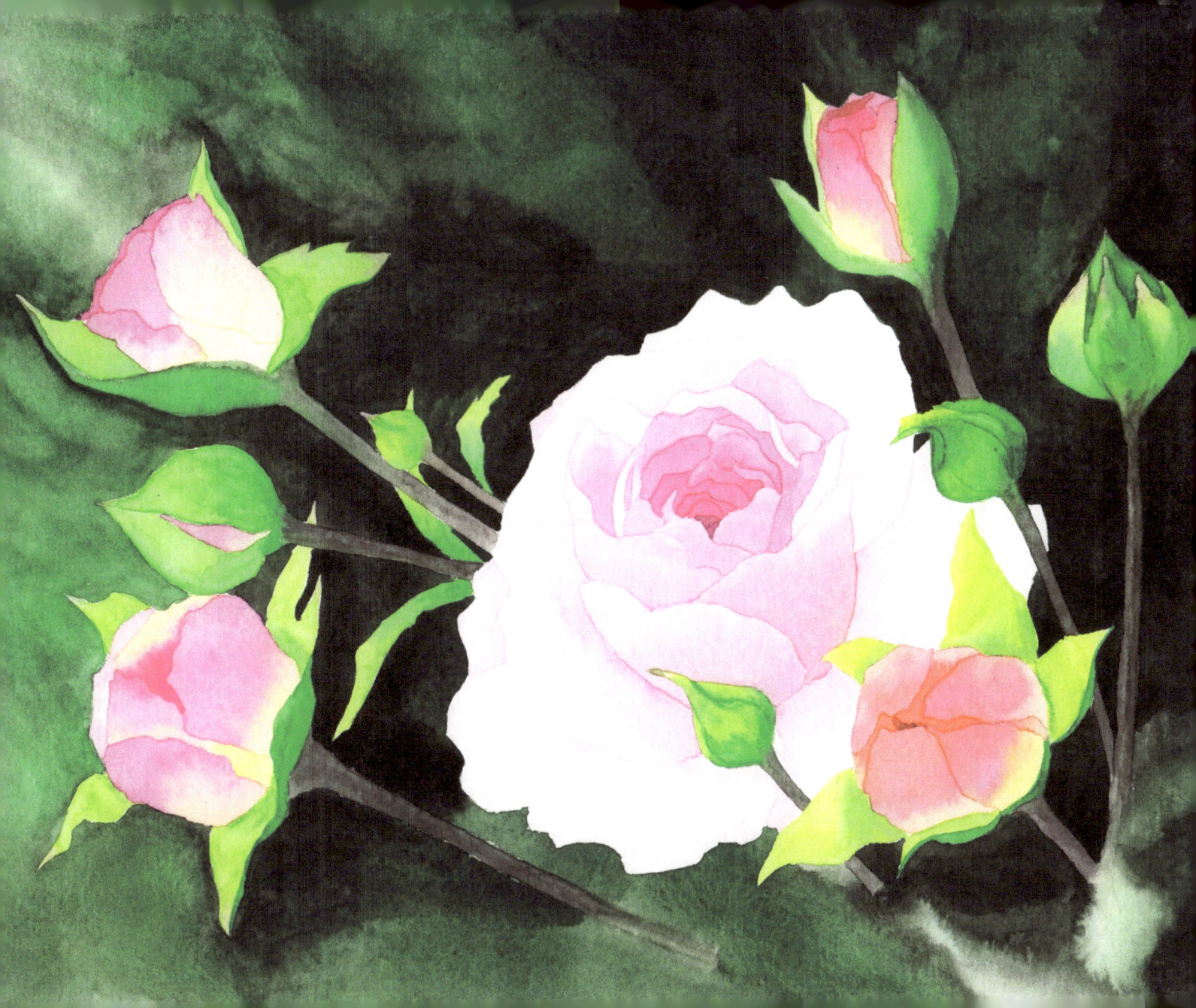

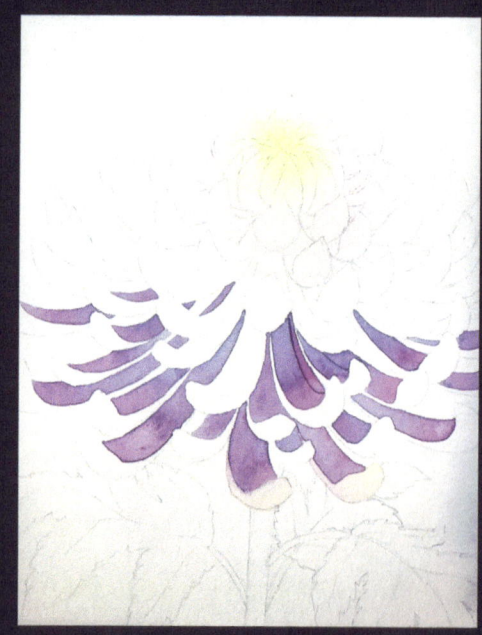

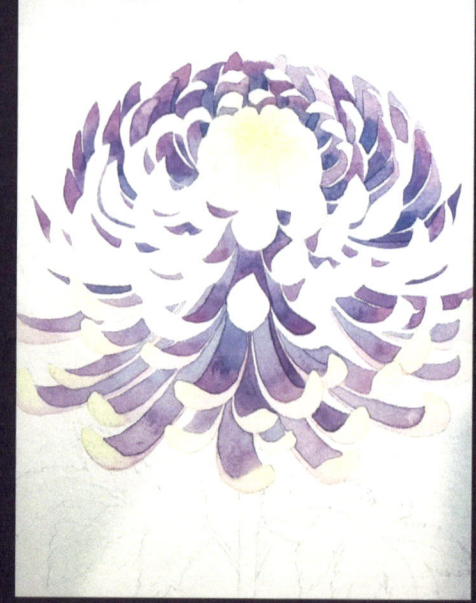

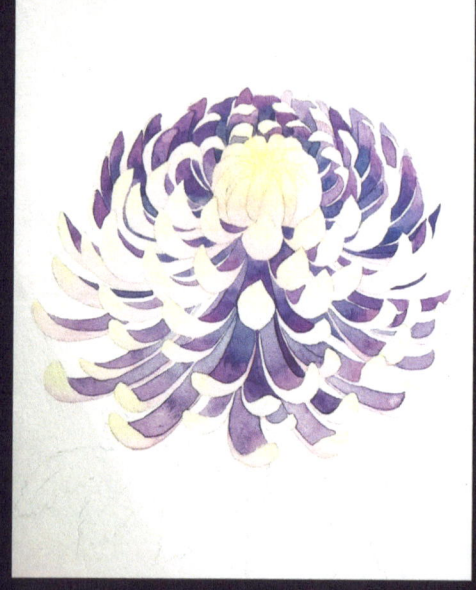

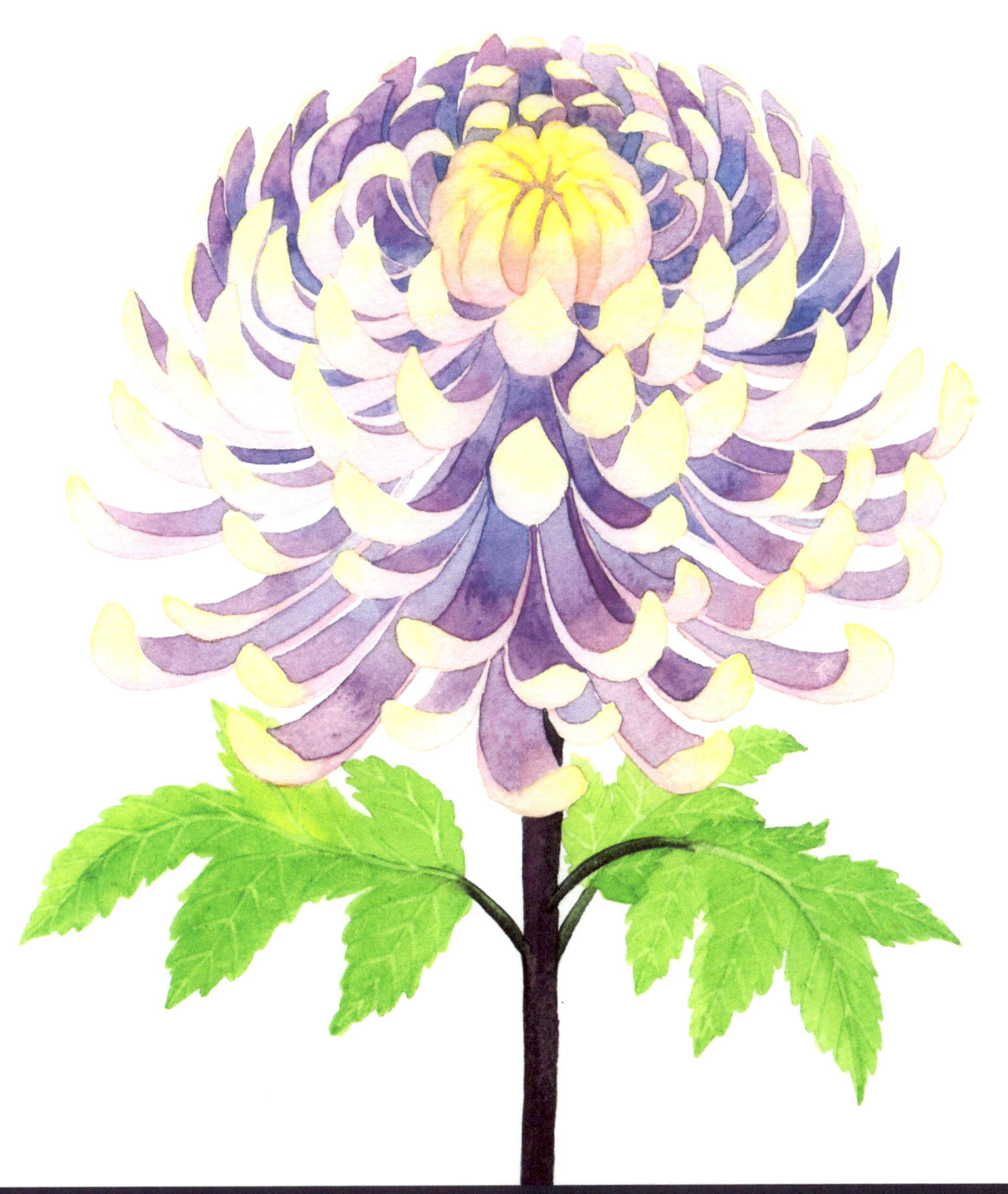

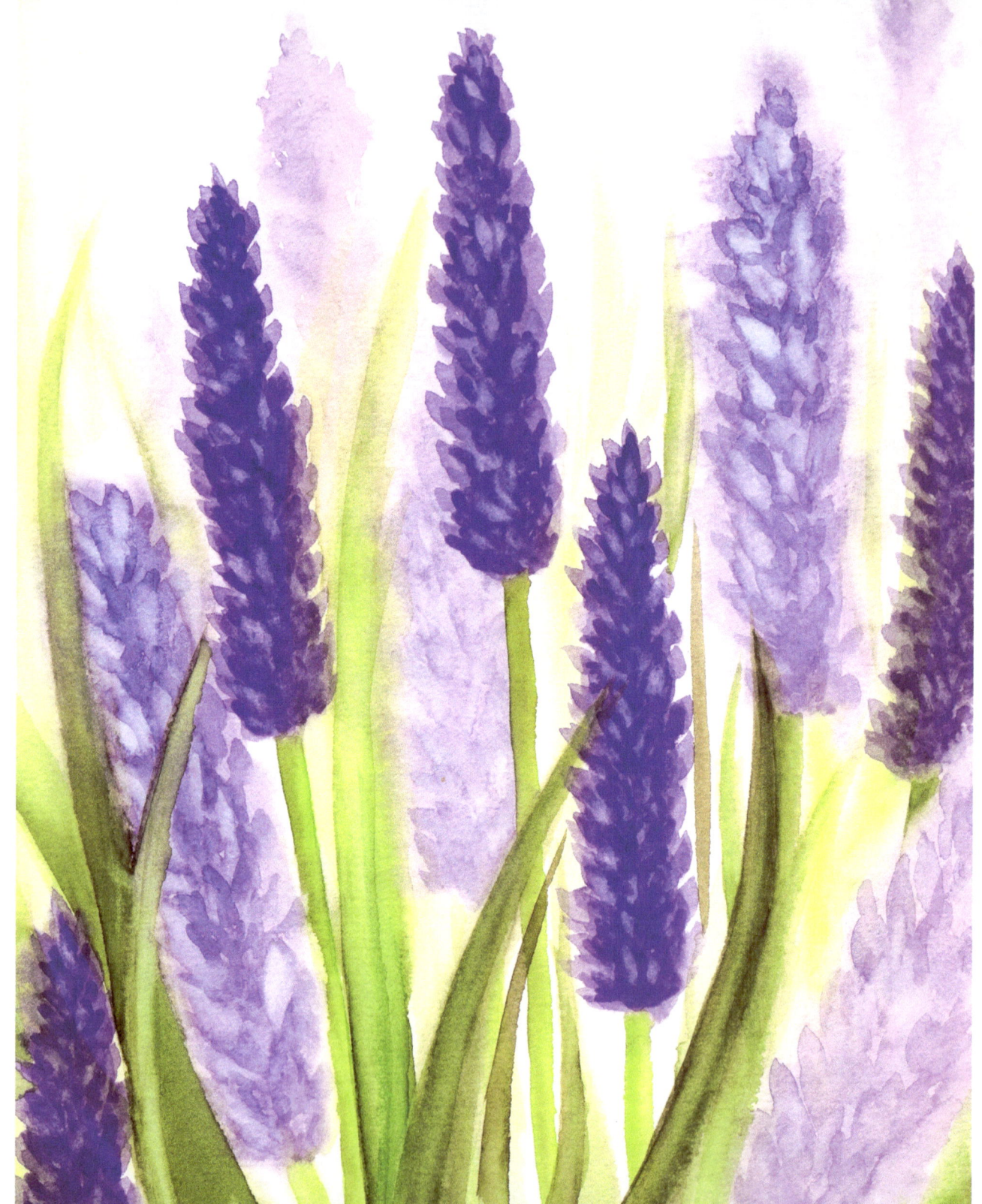

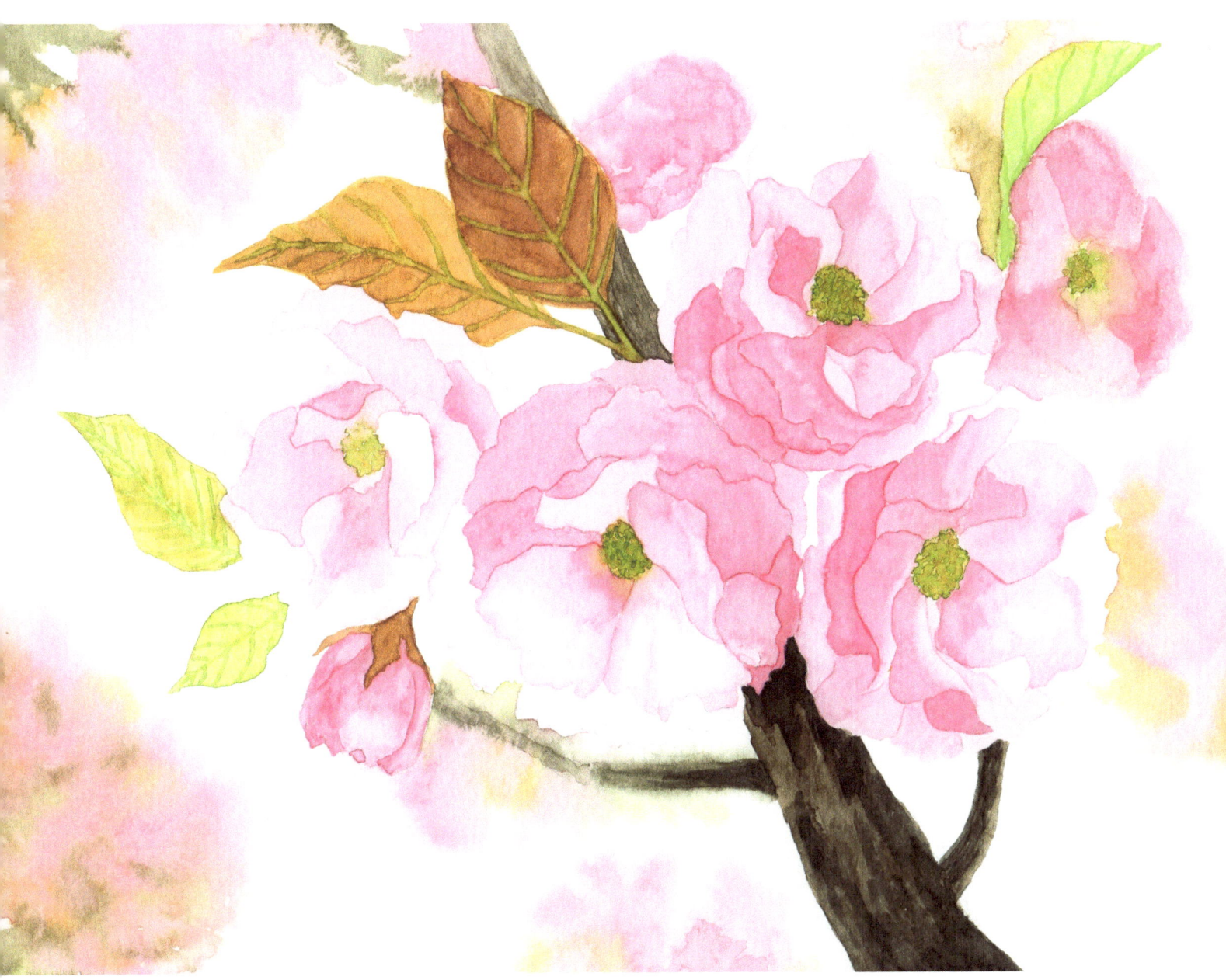

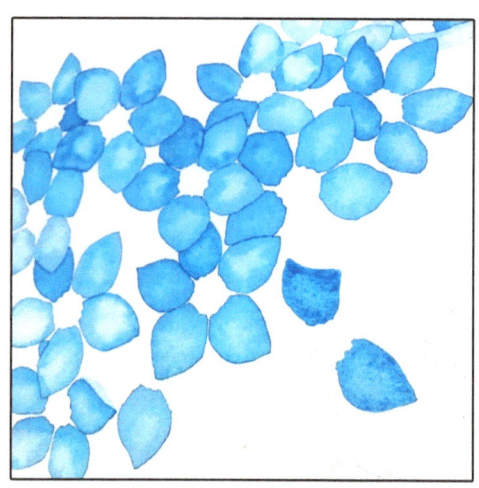

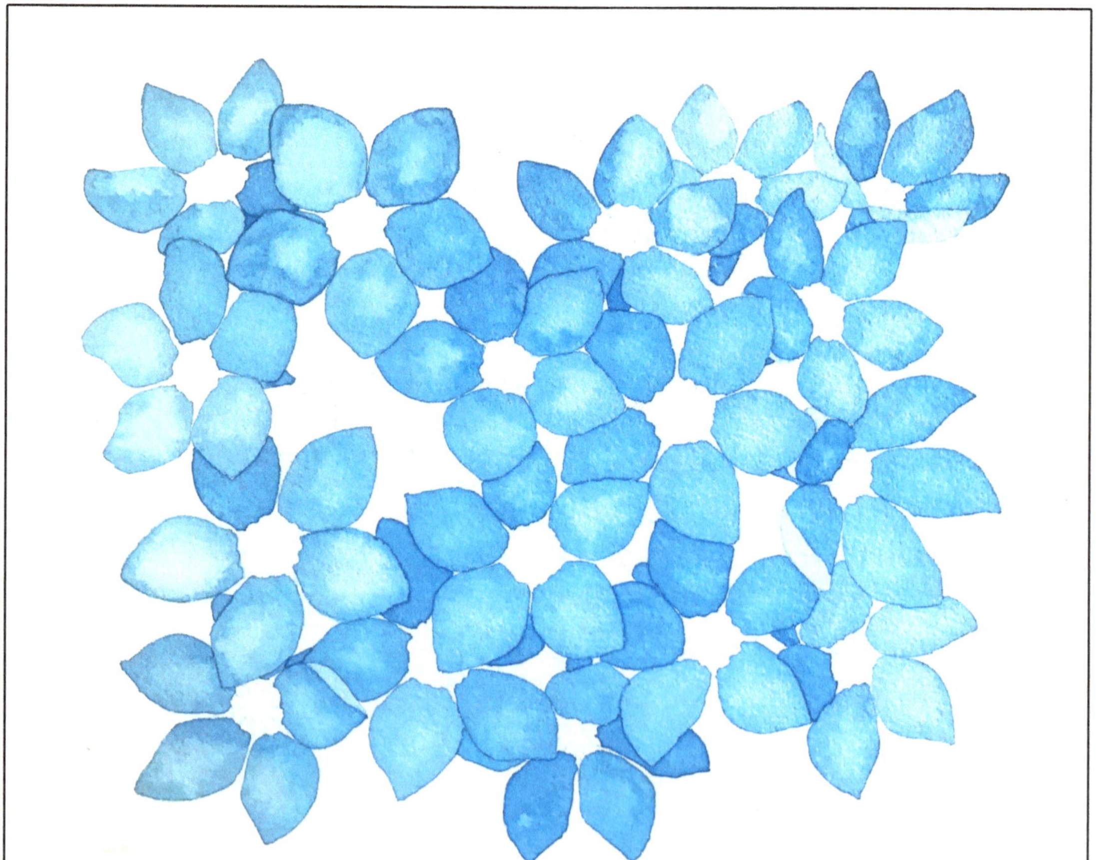

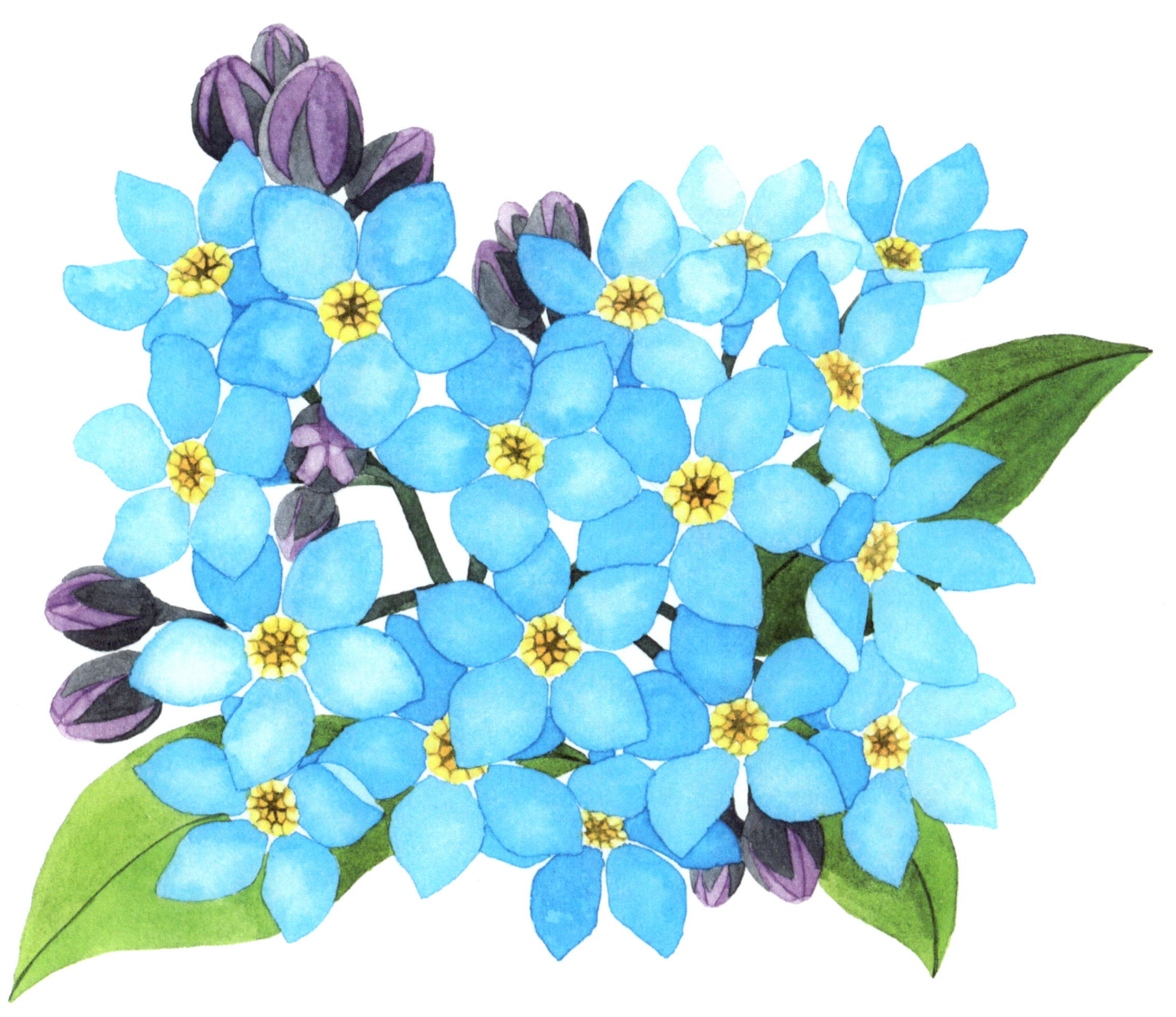

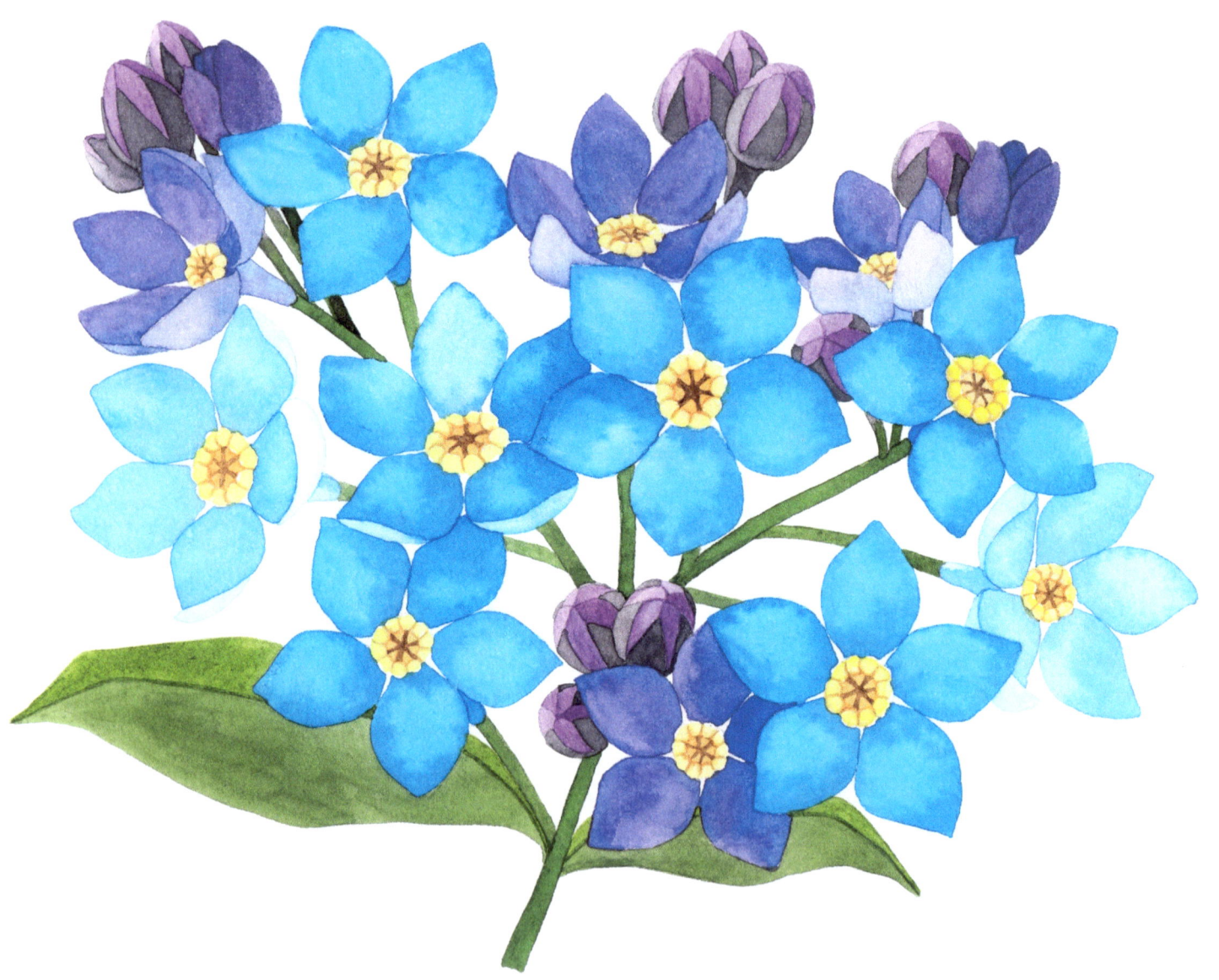

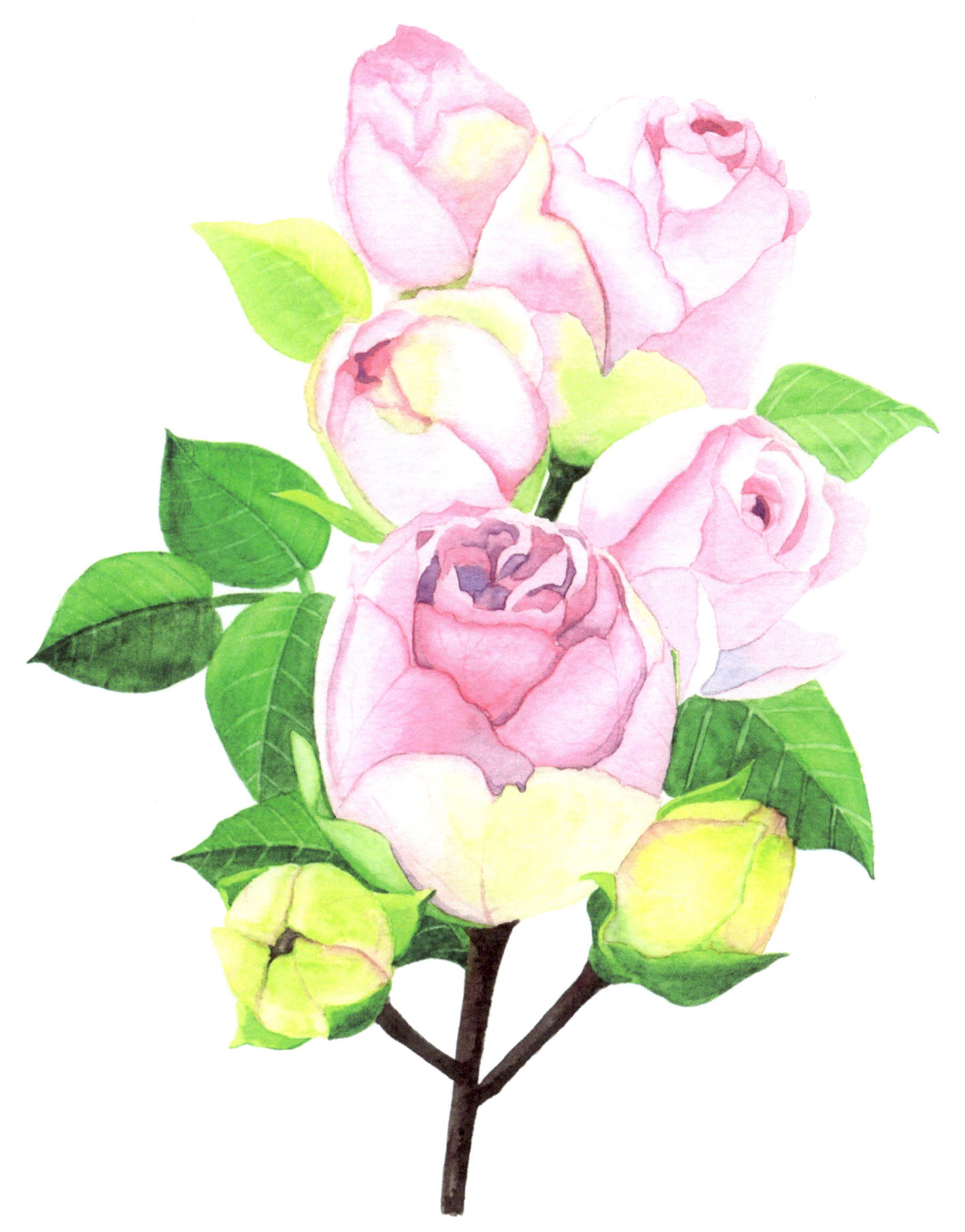

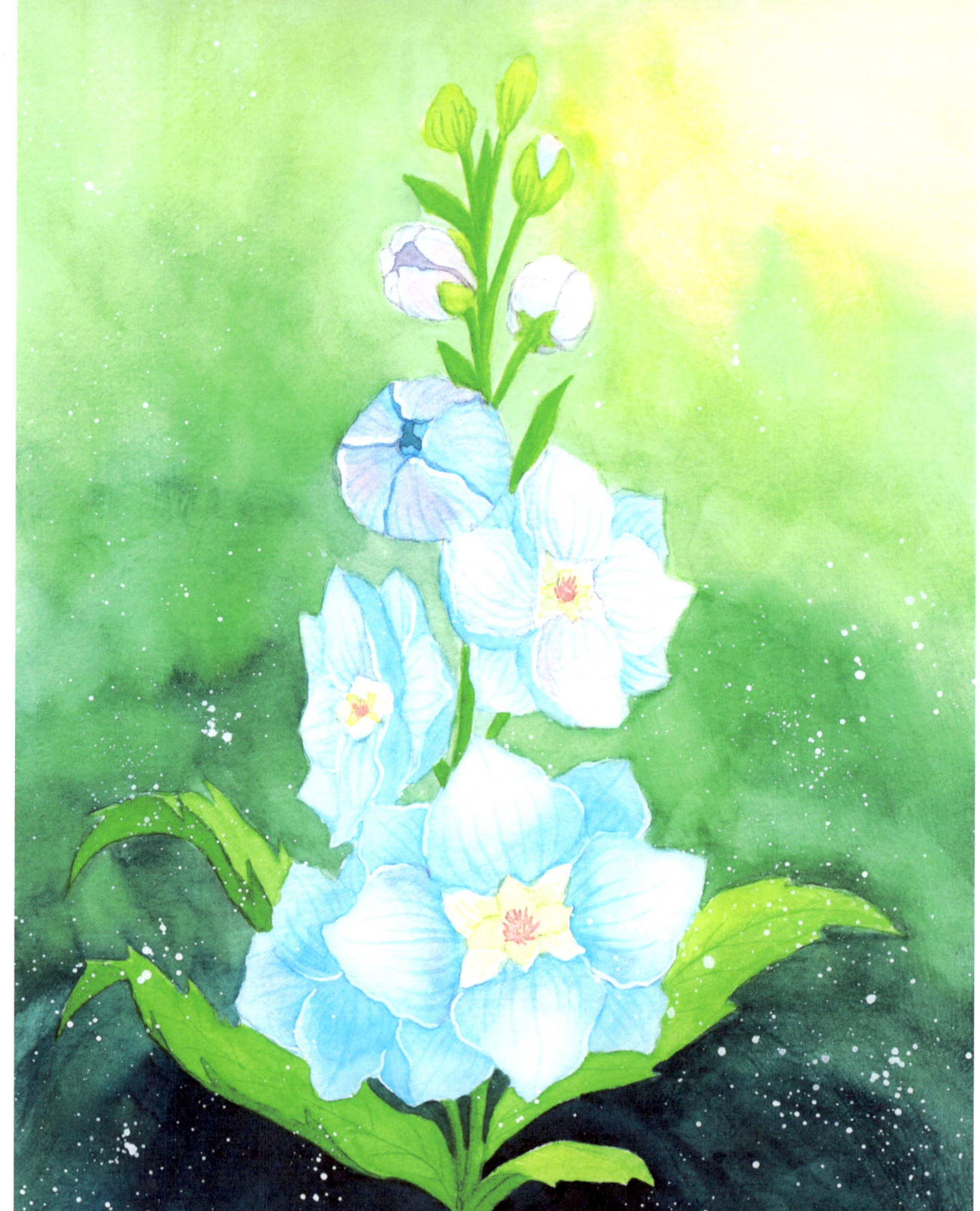

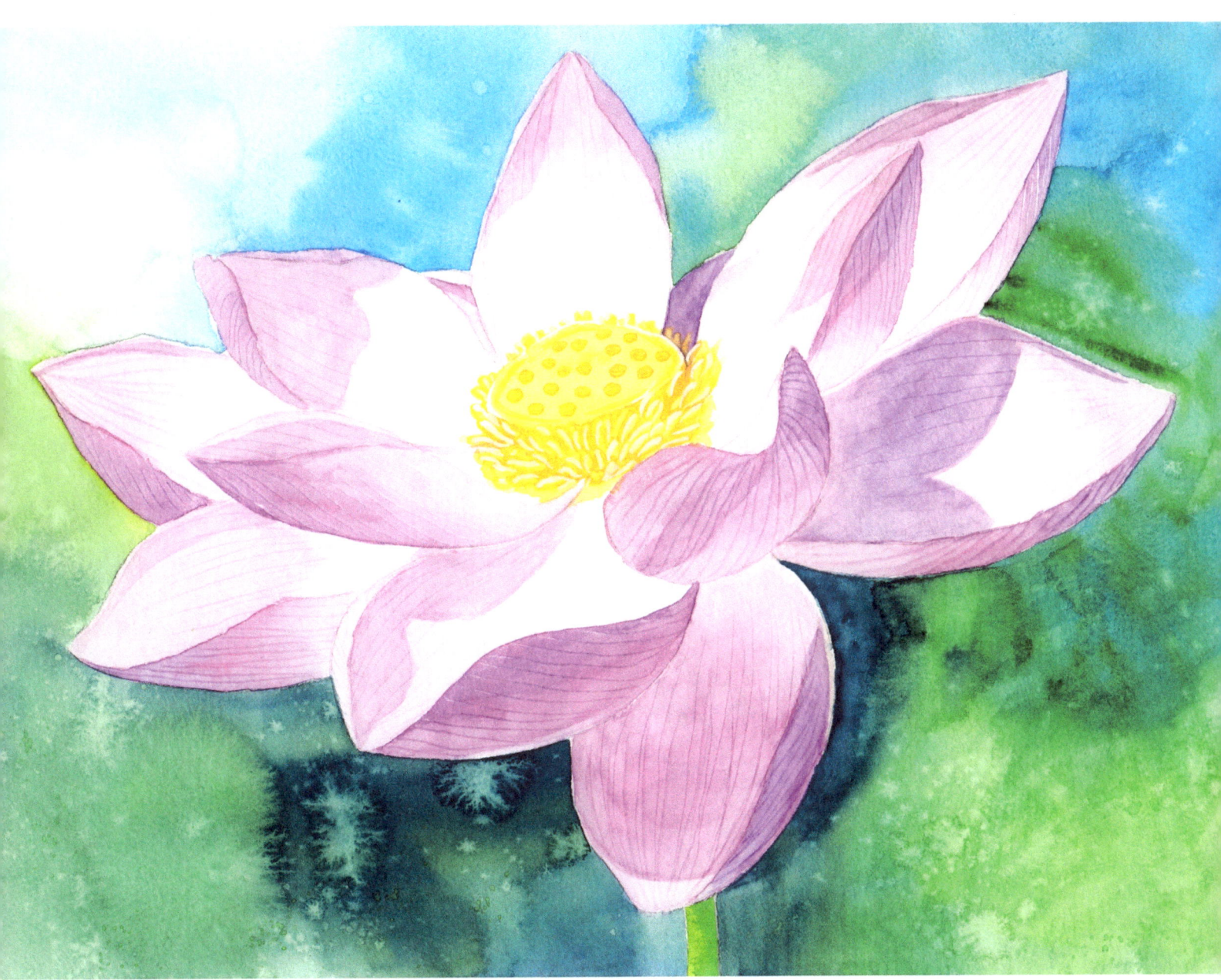

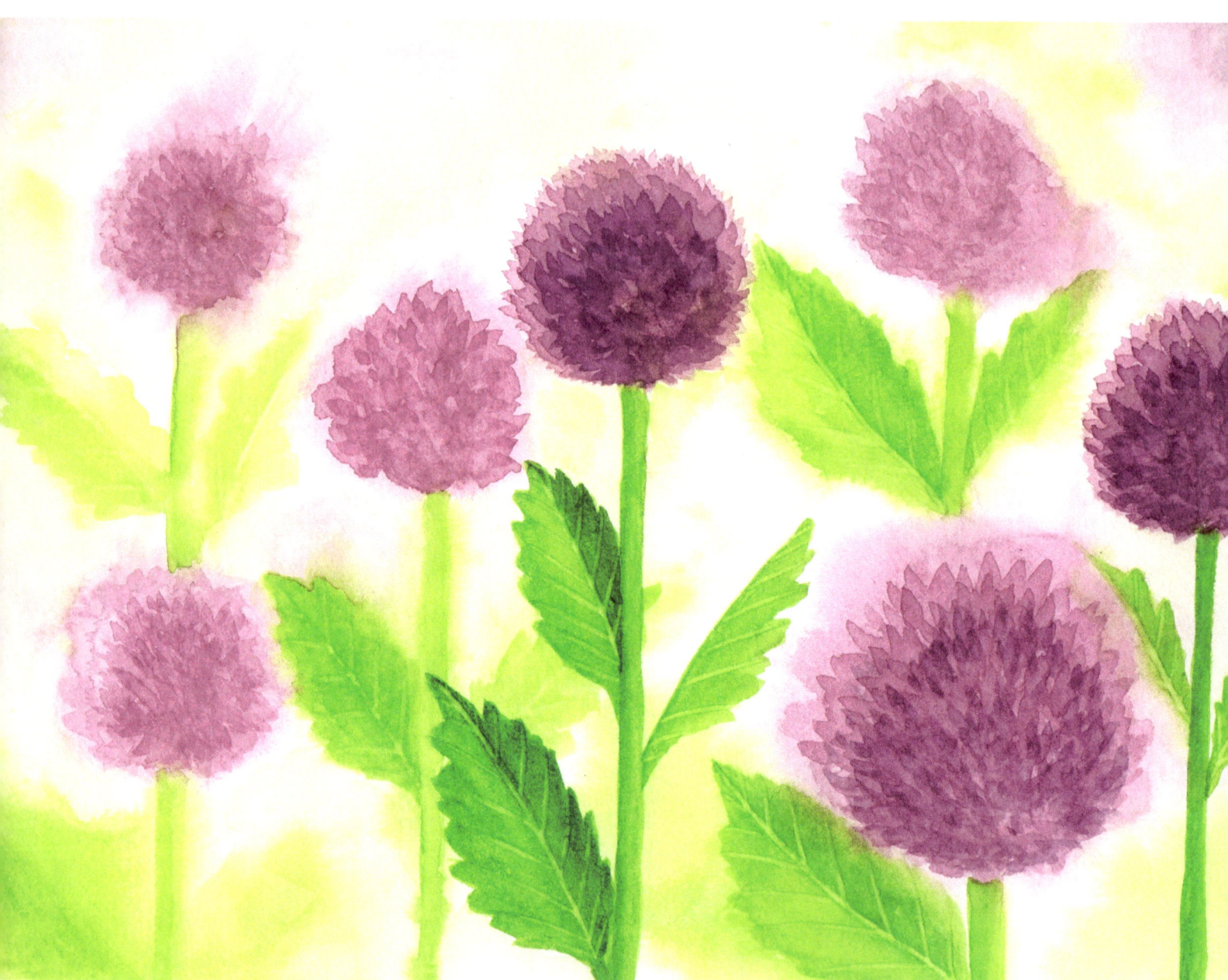

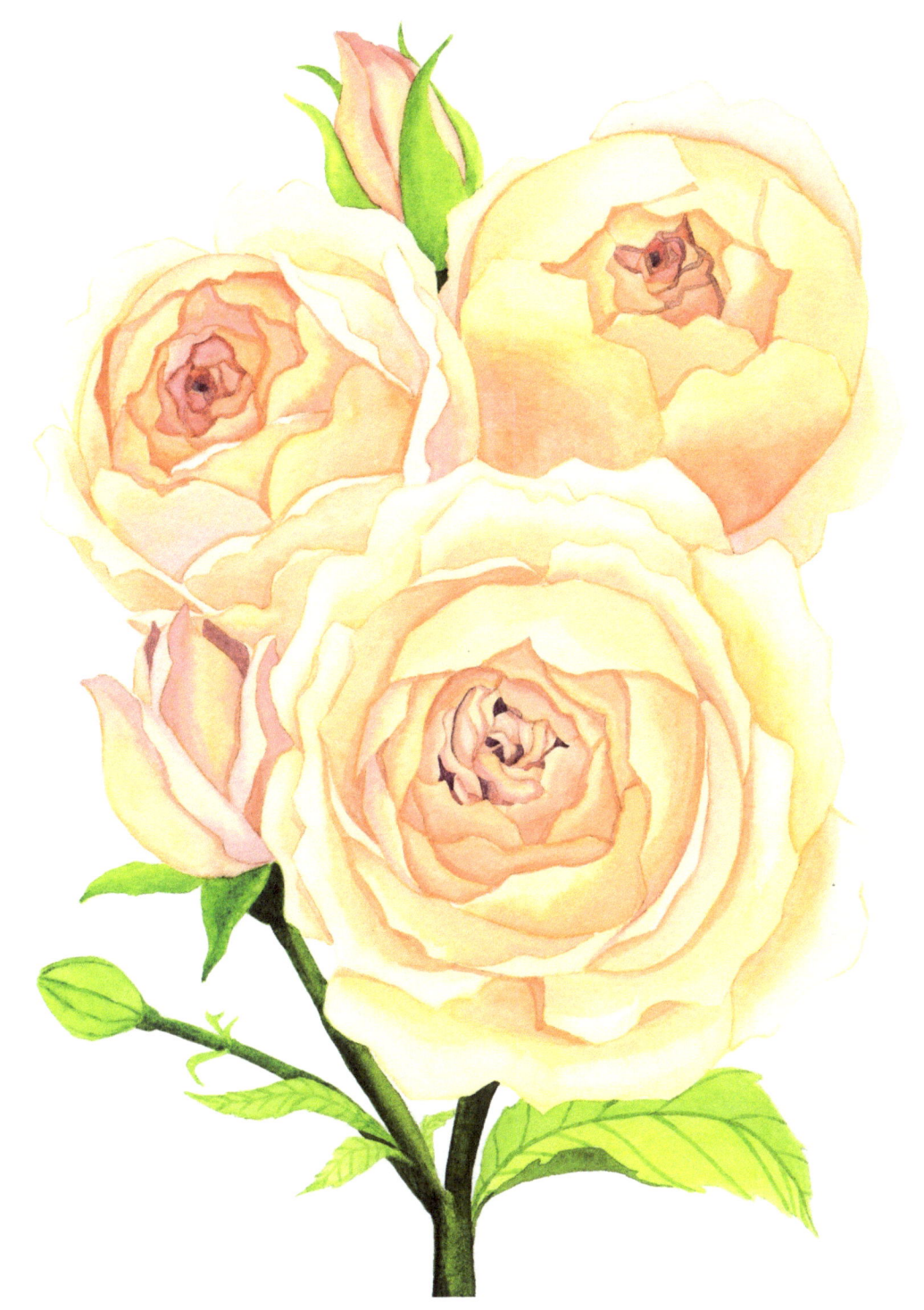

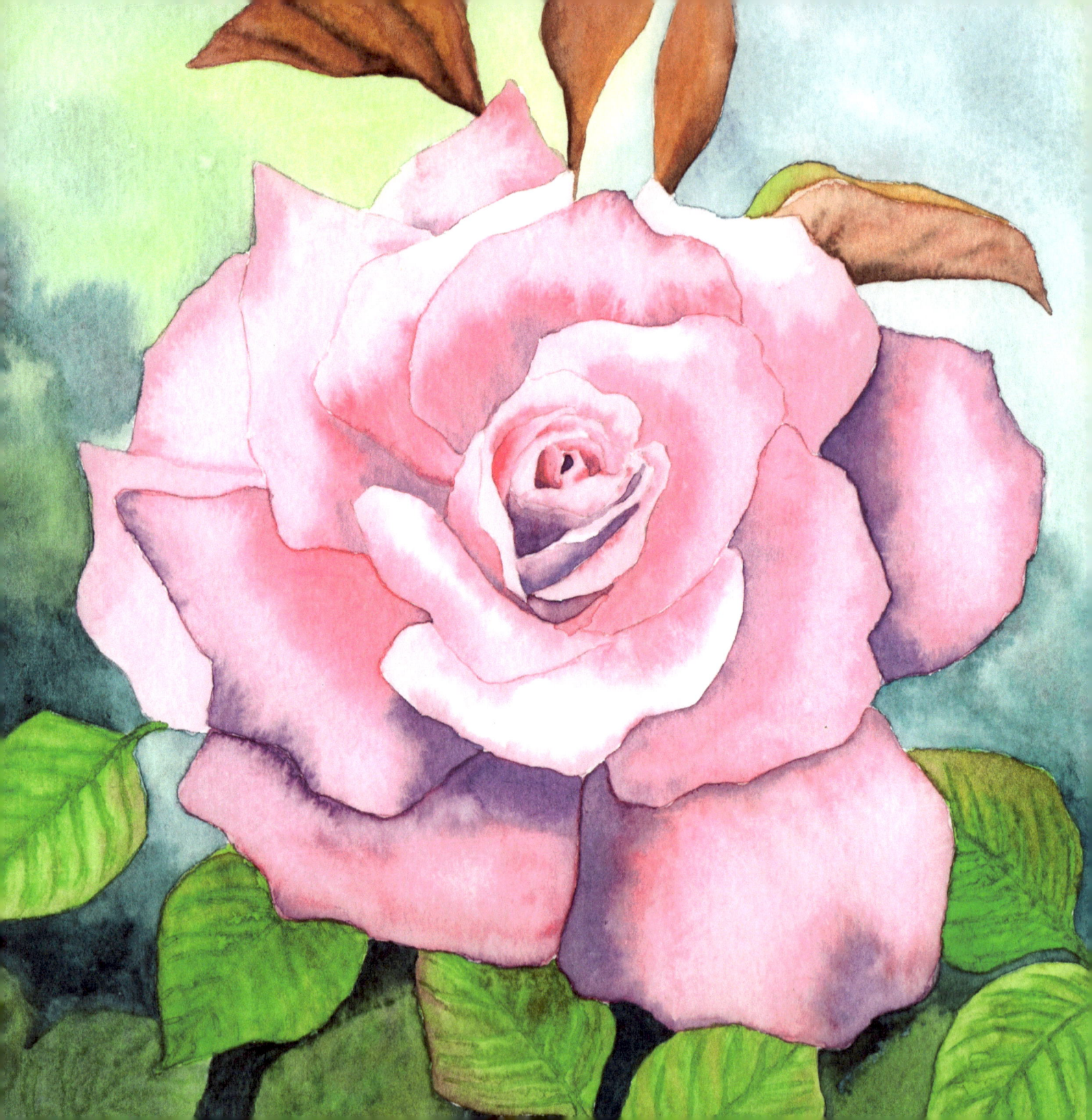

Asian Landscapes 景

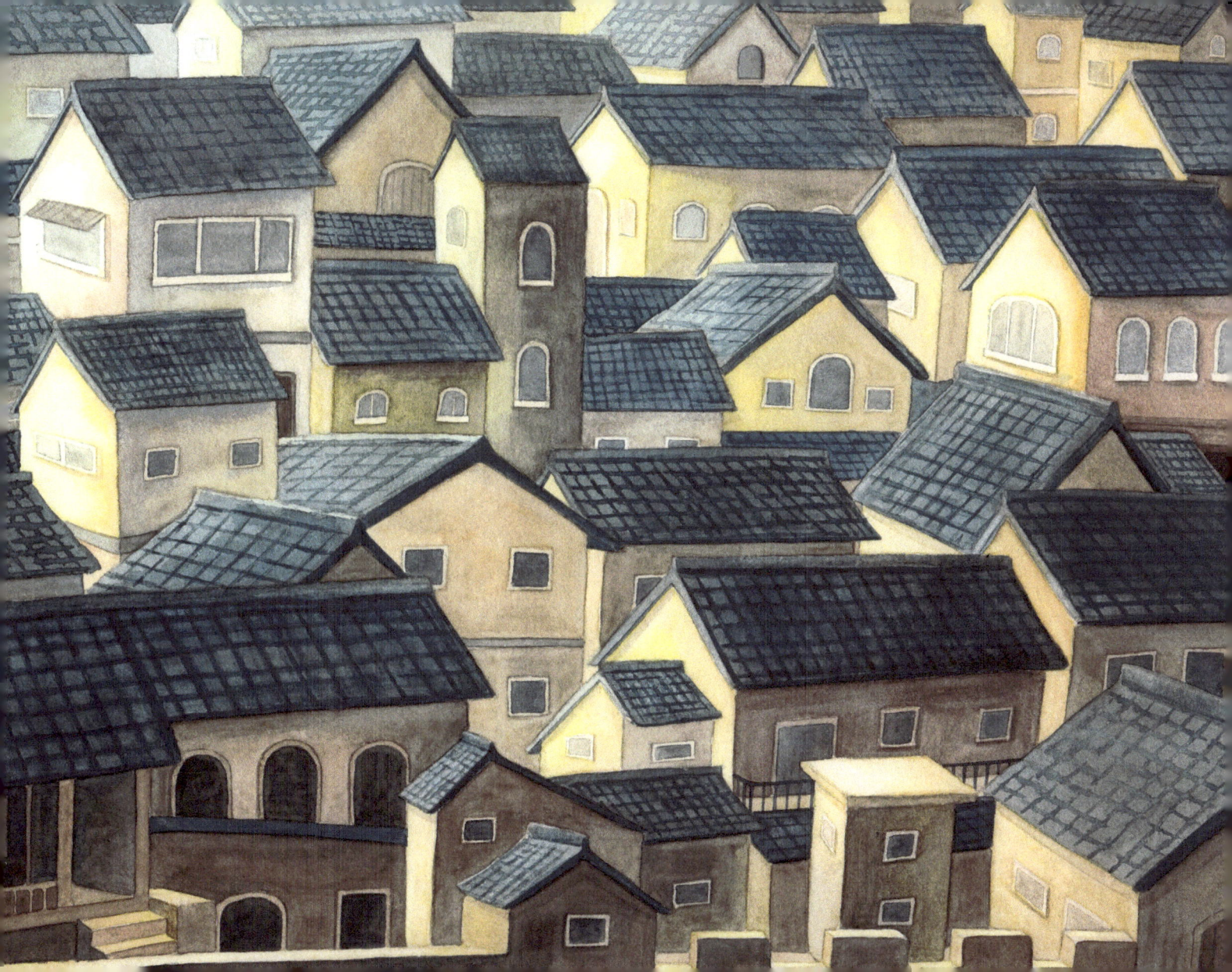

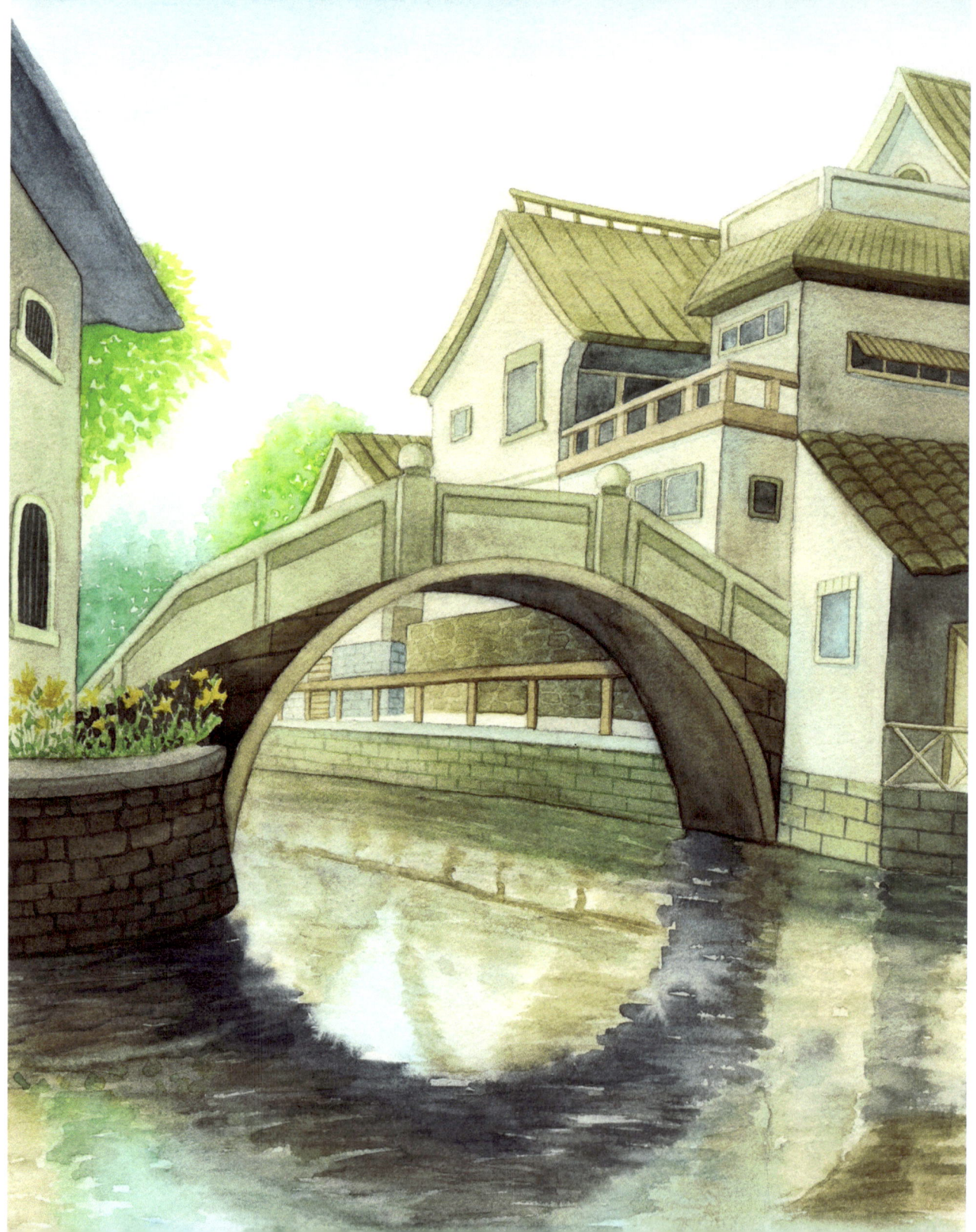

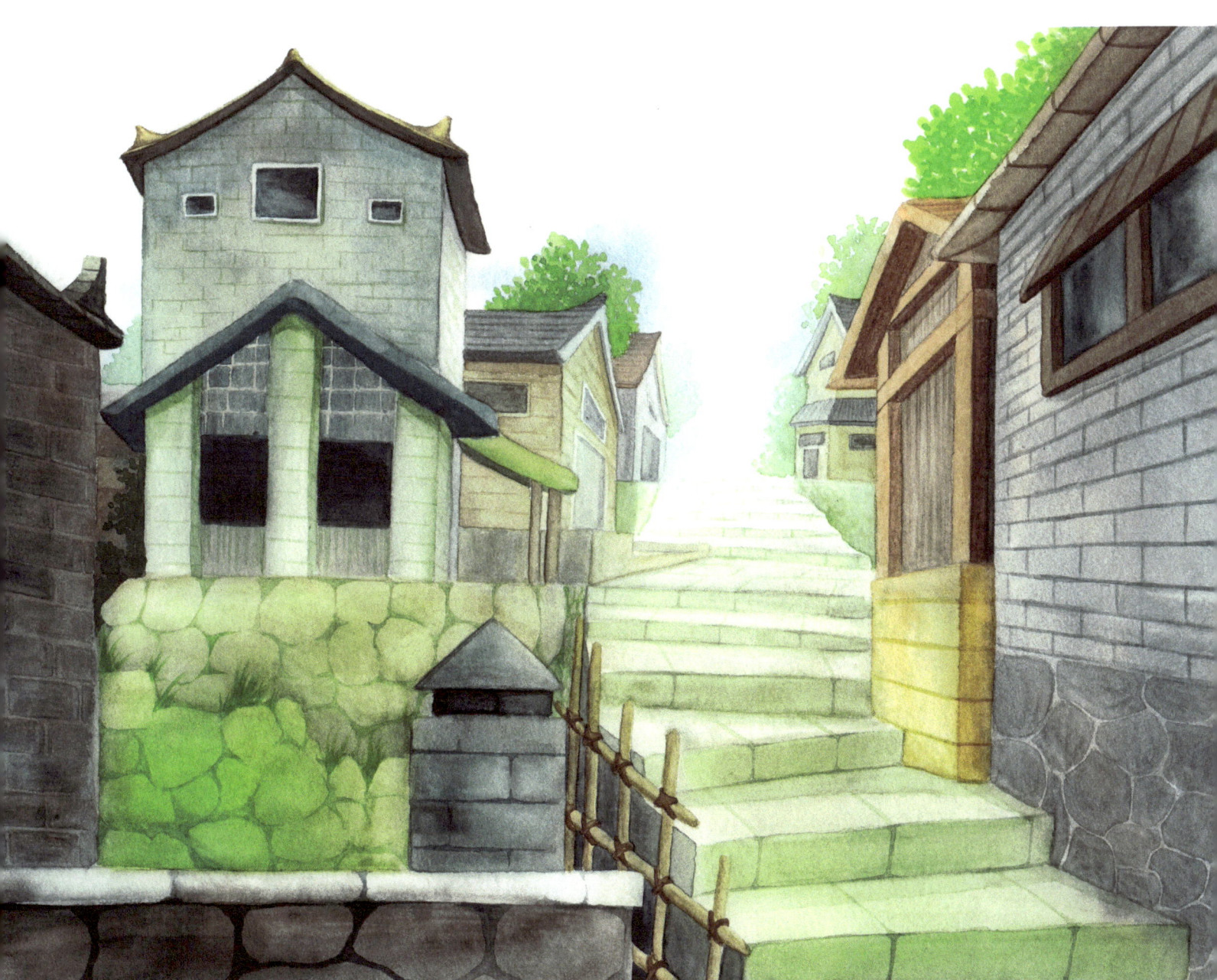

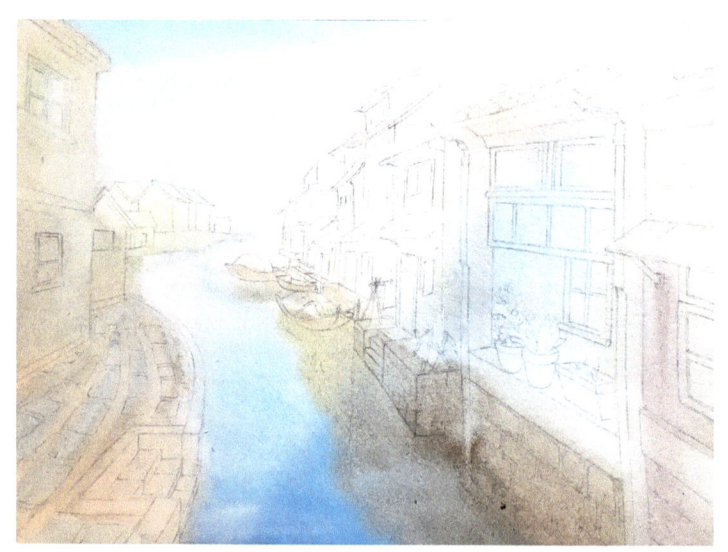

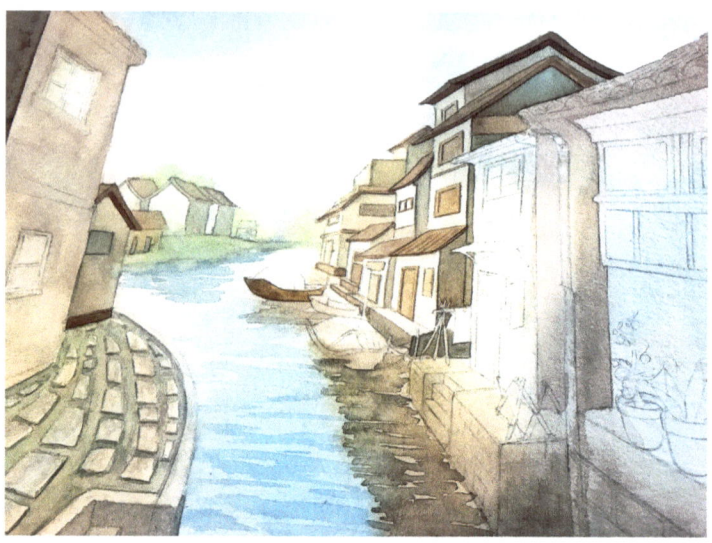

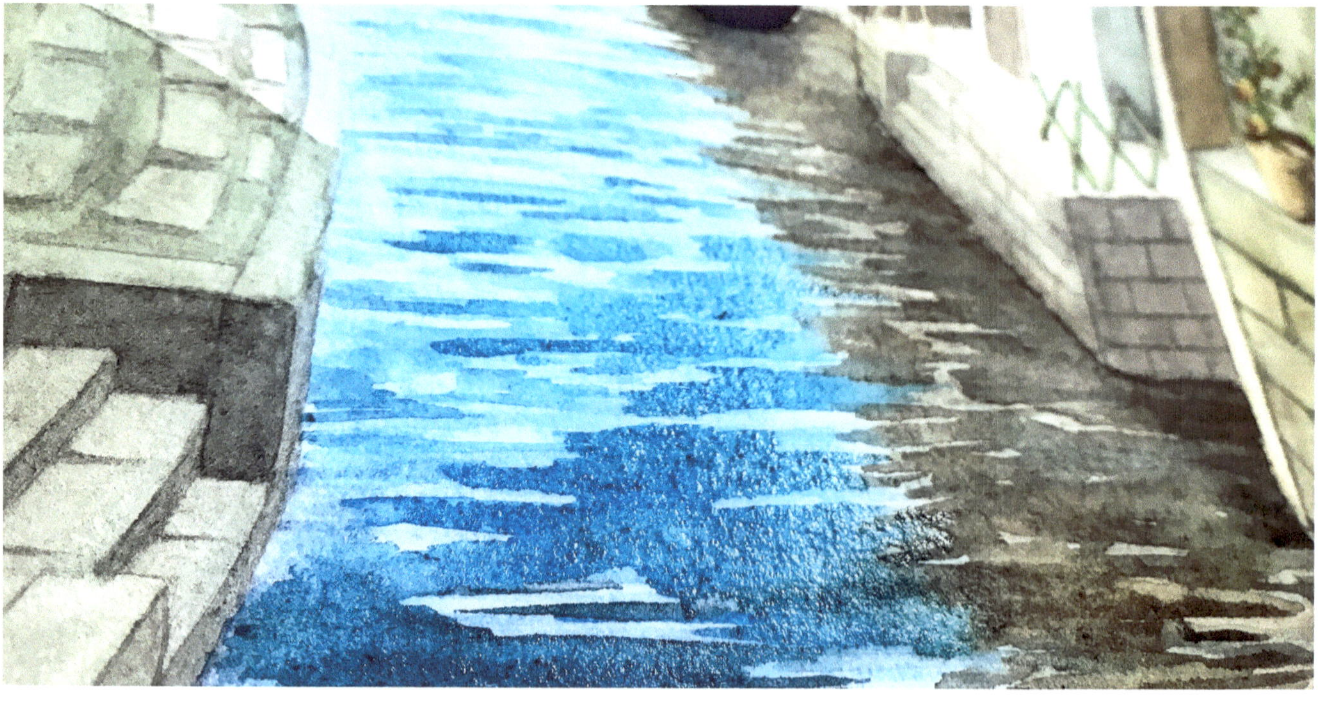

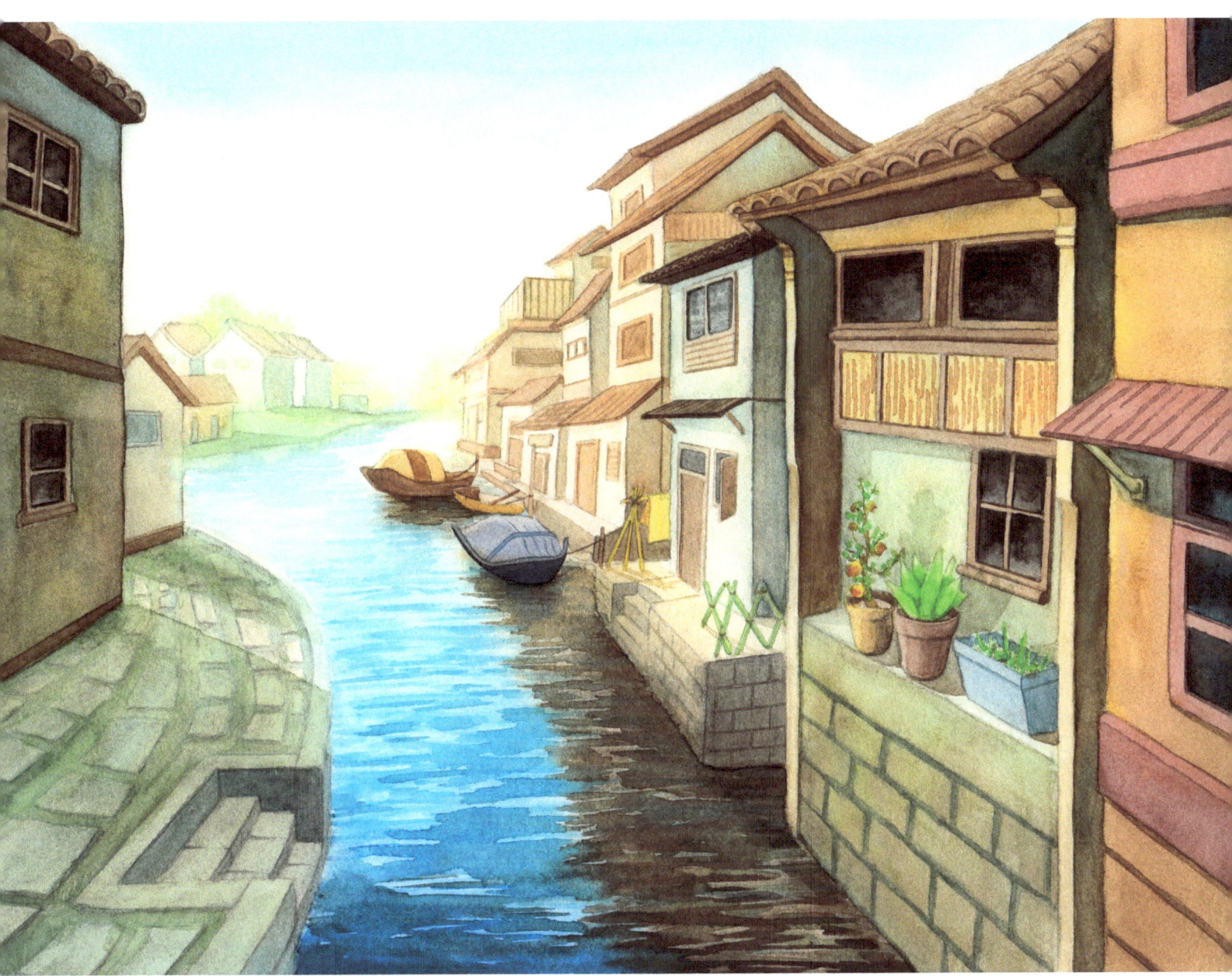

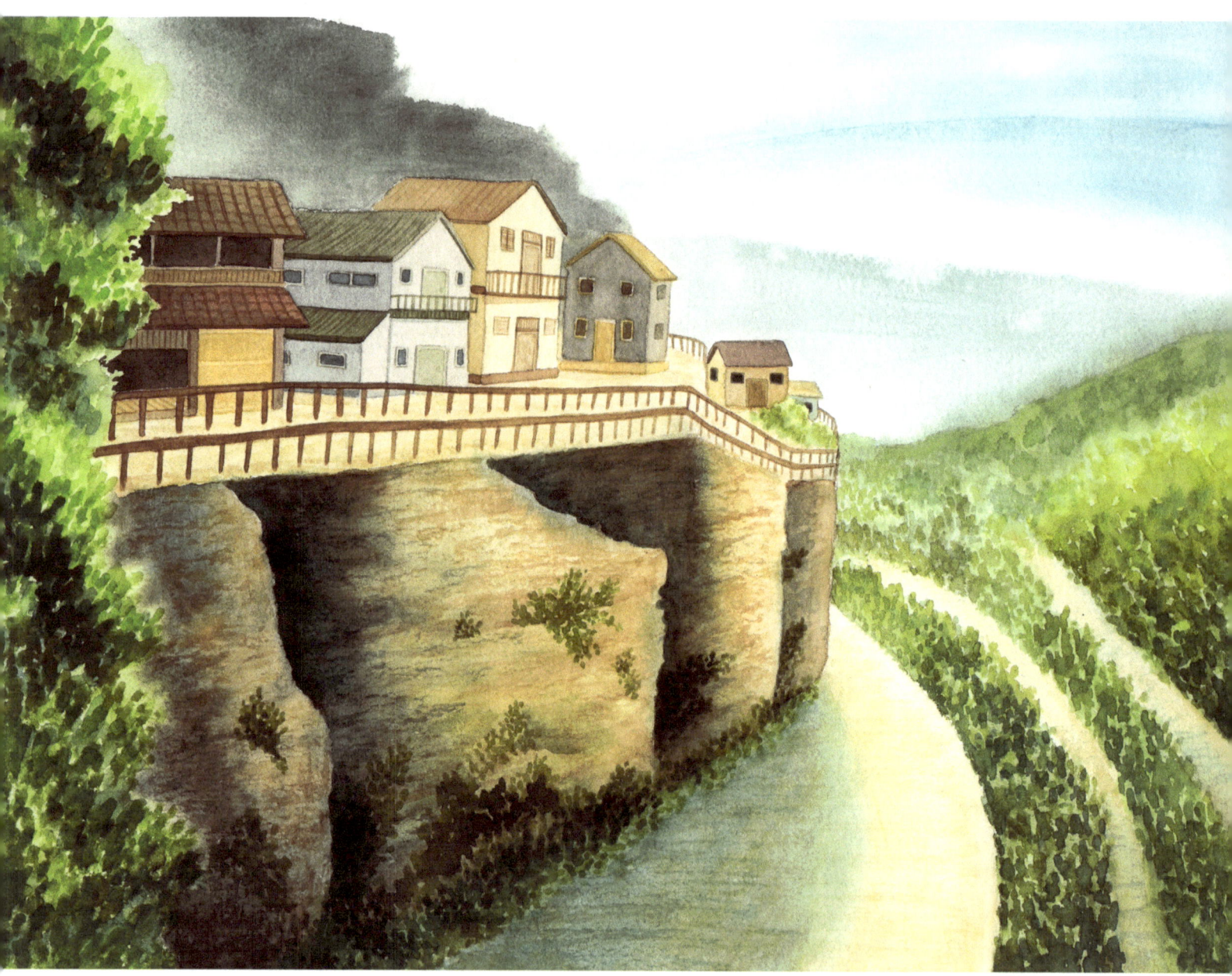

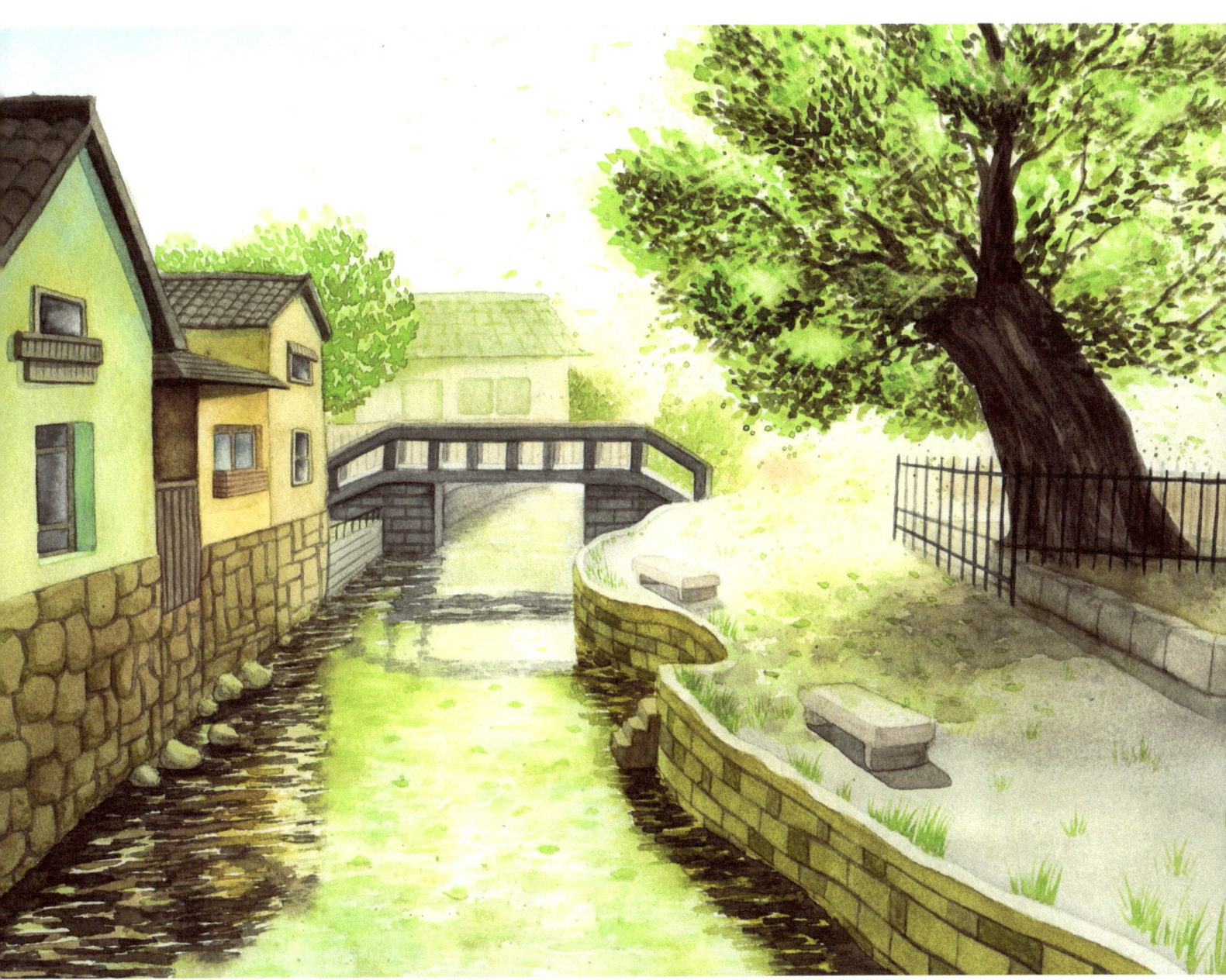

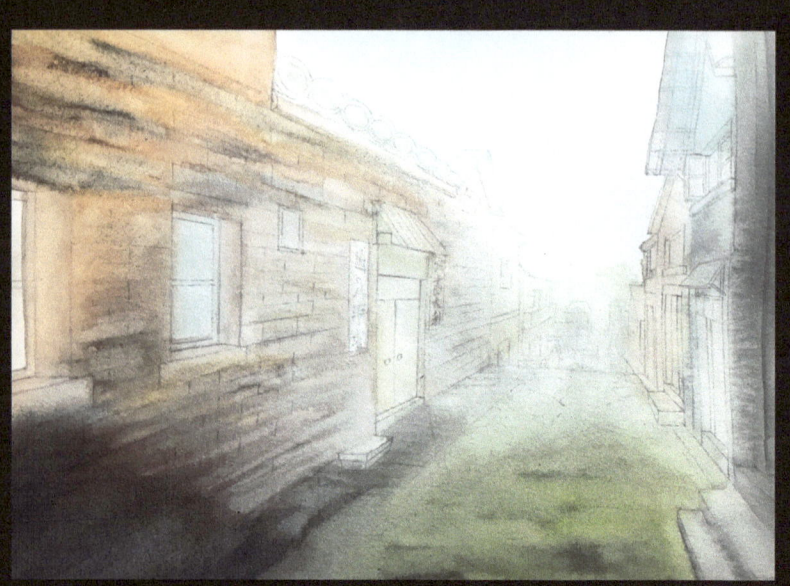

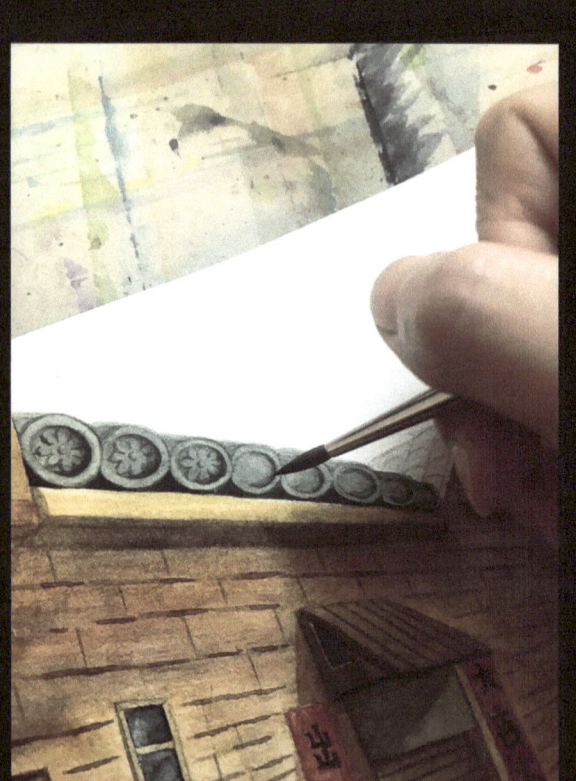

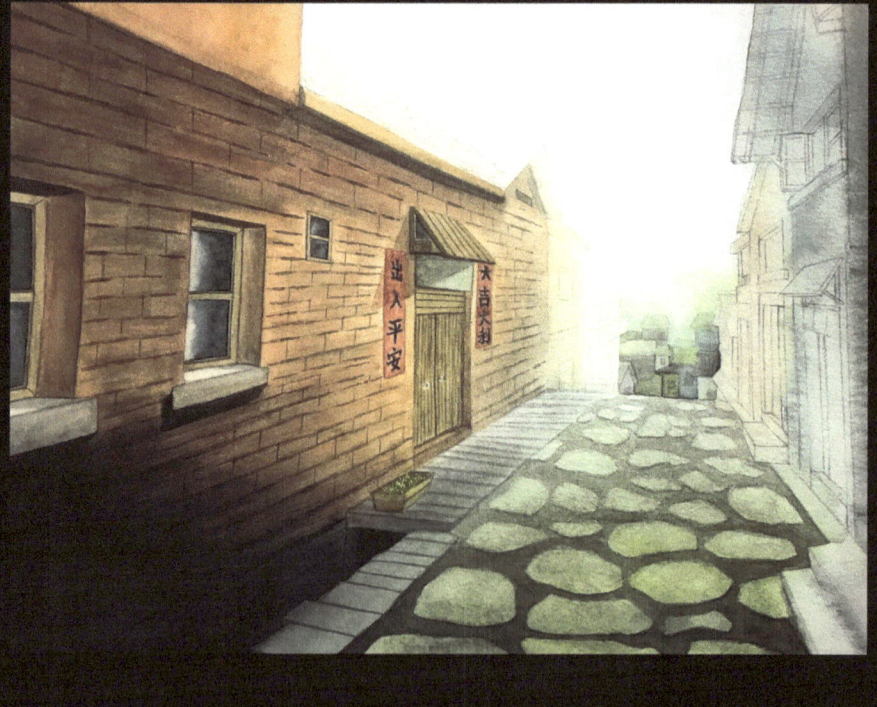

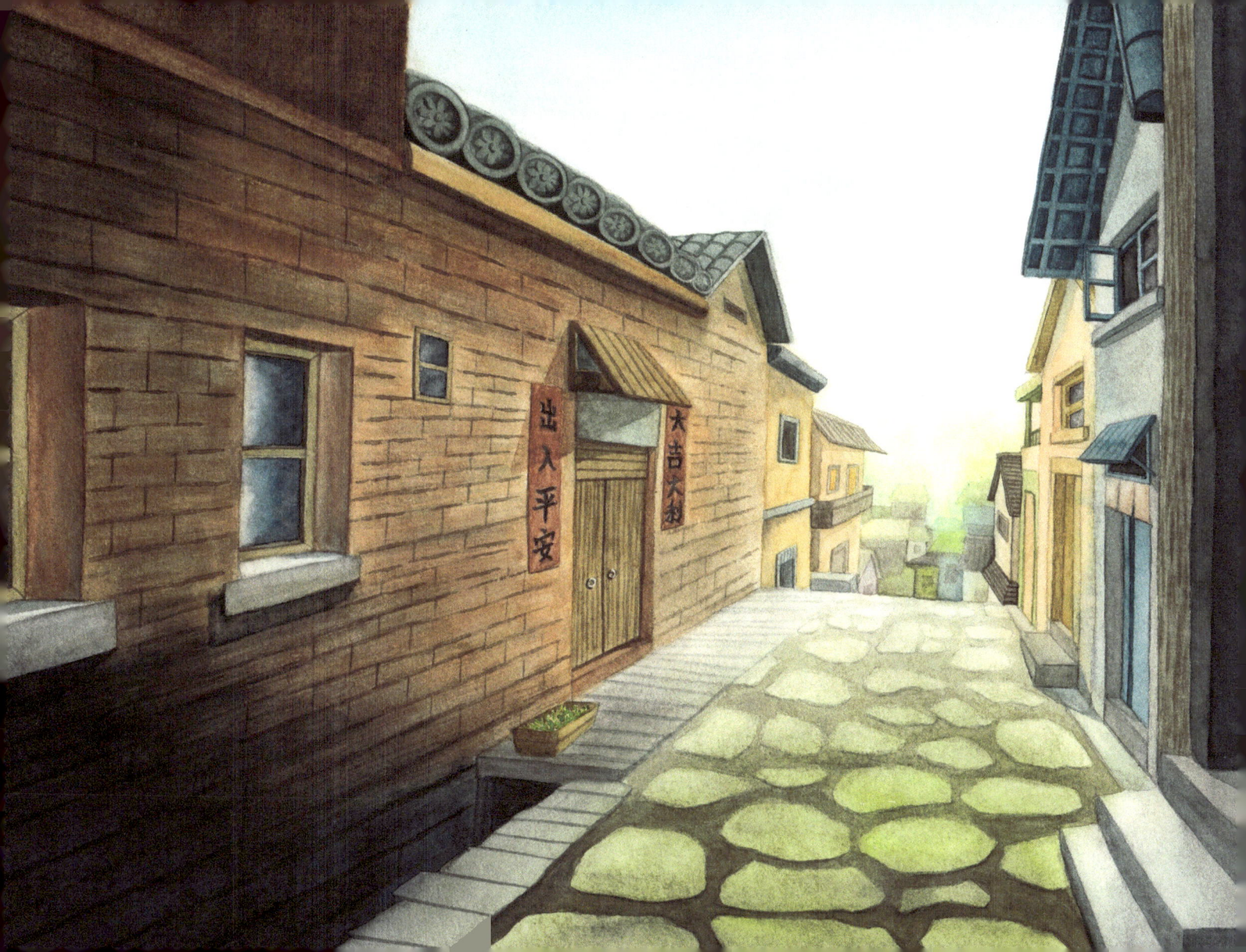

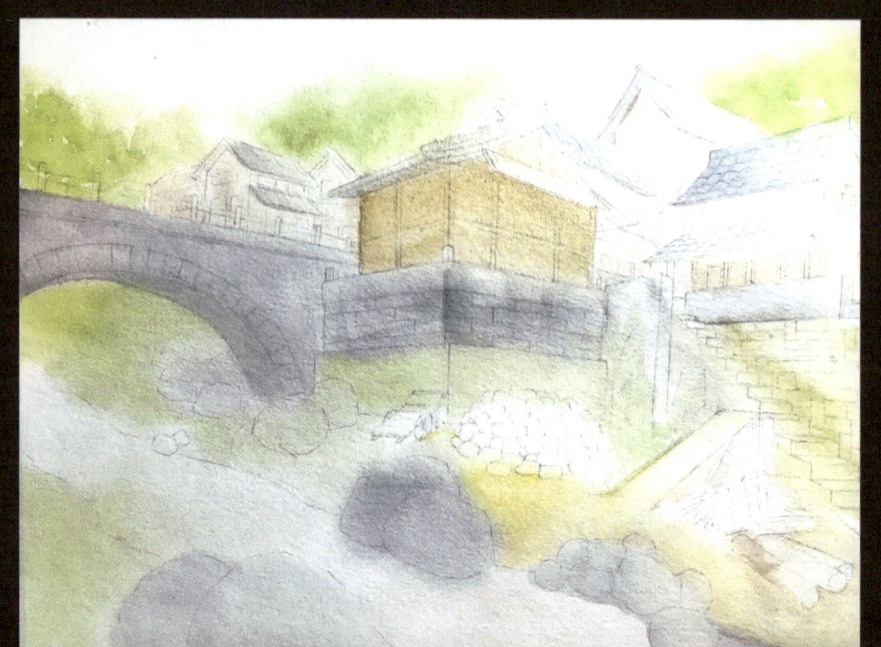
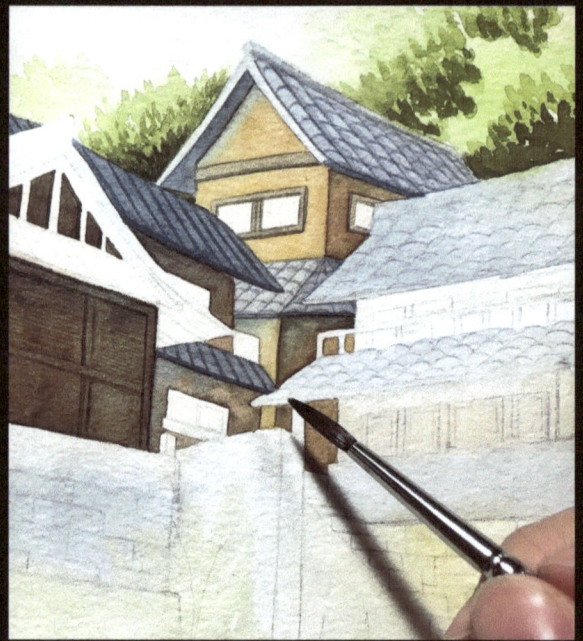

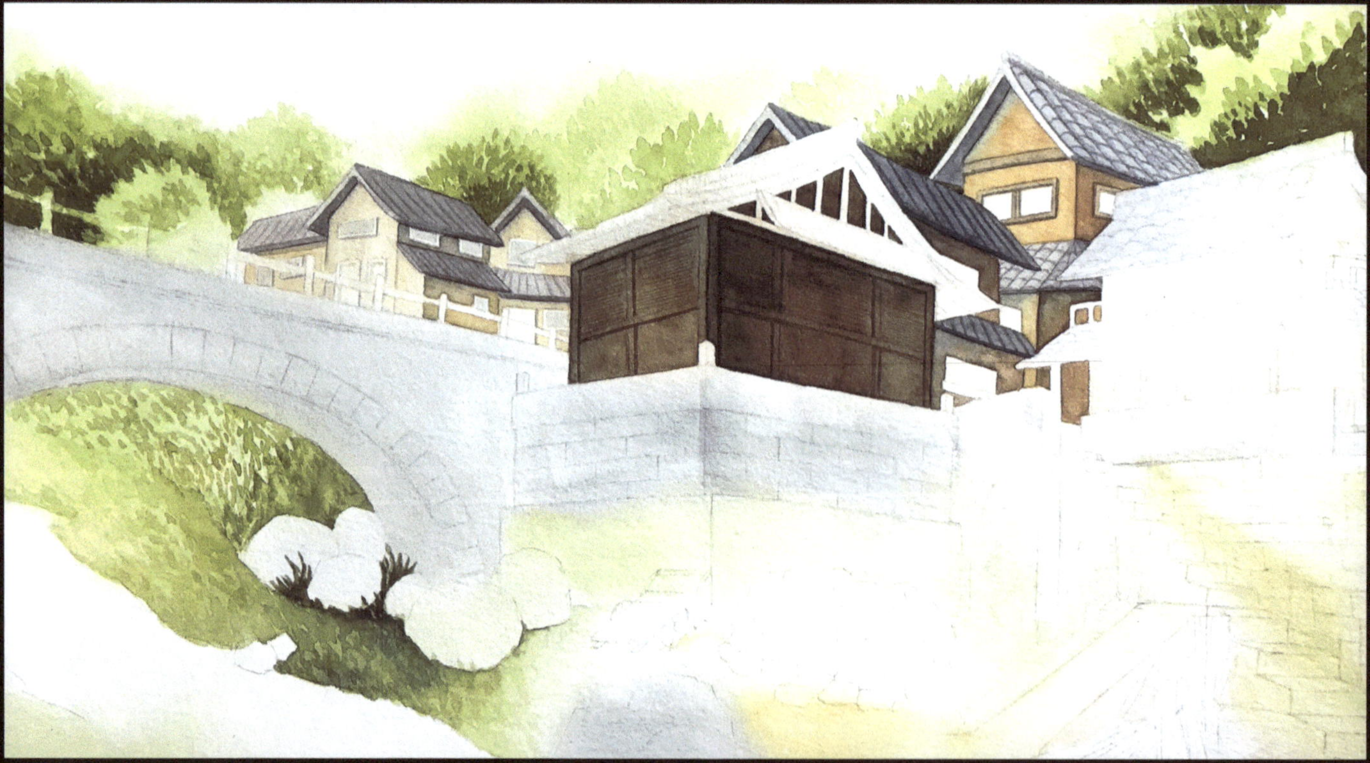

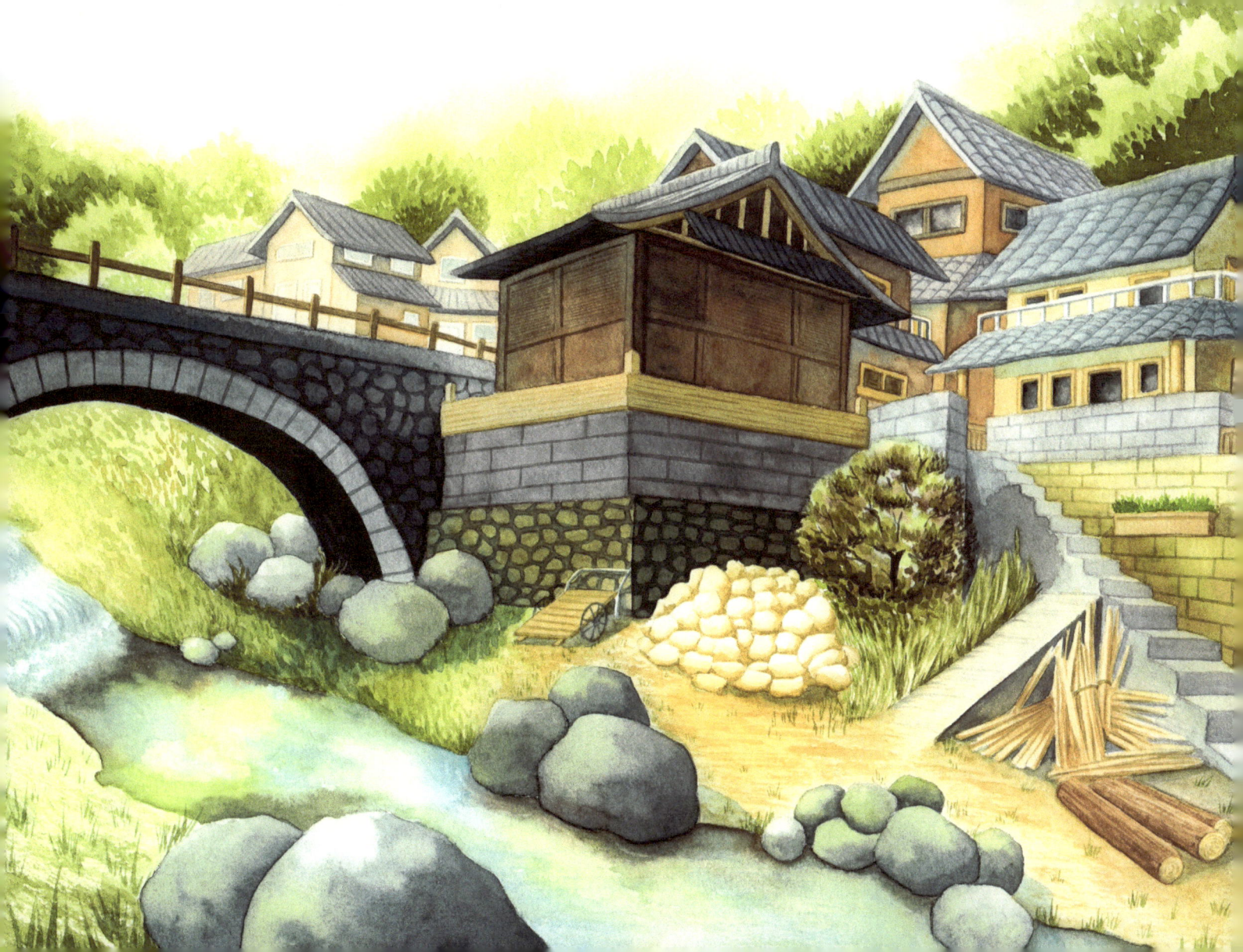

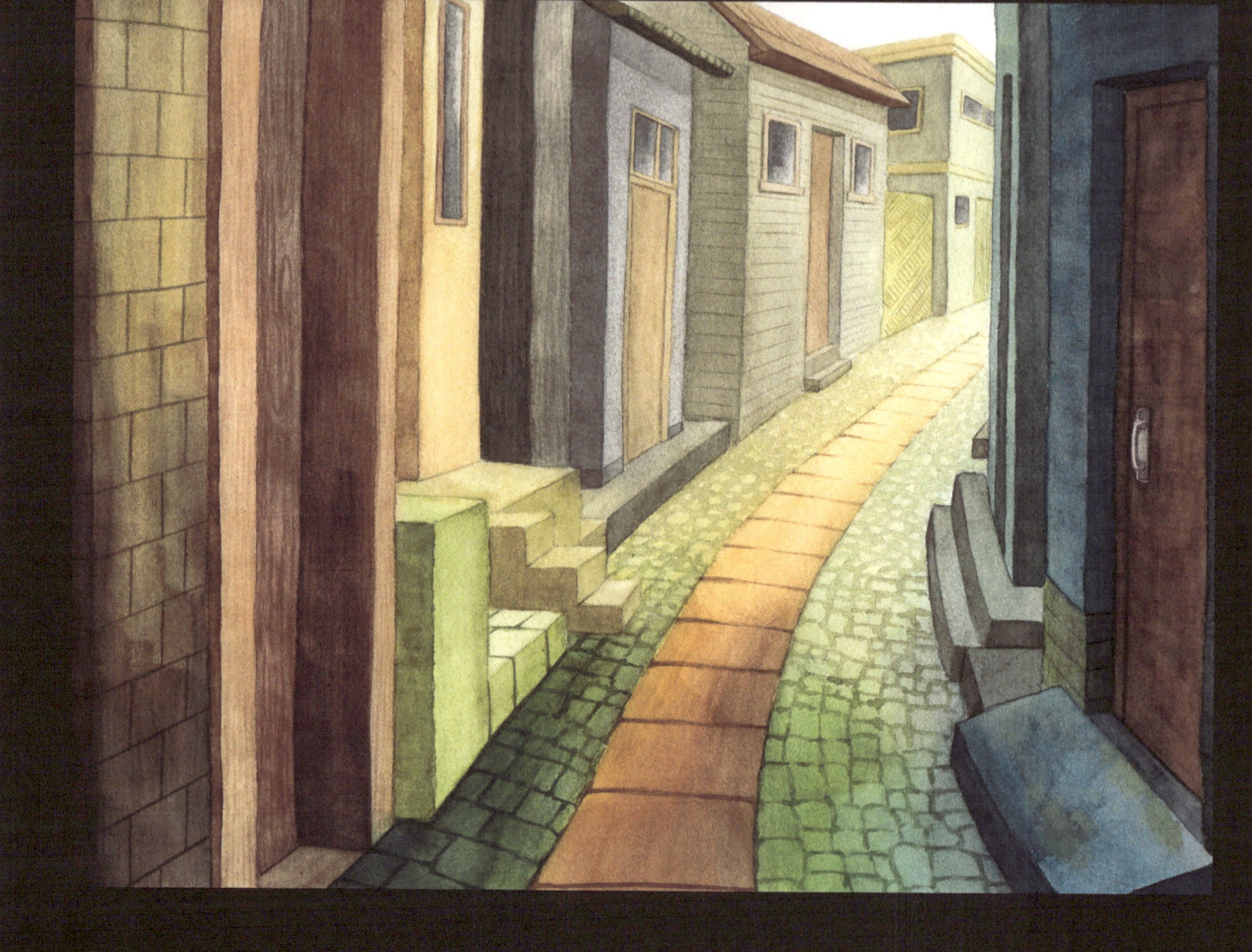

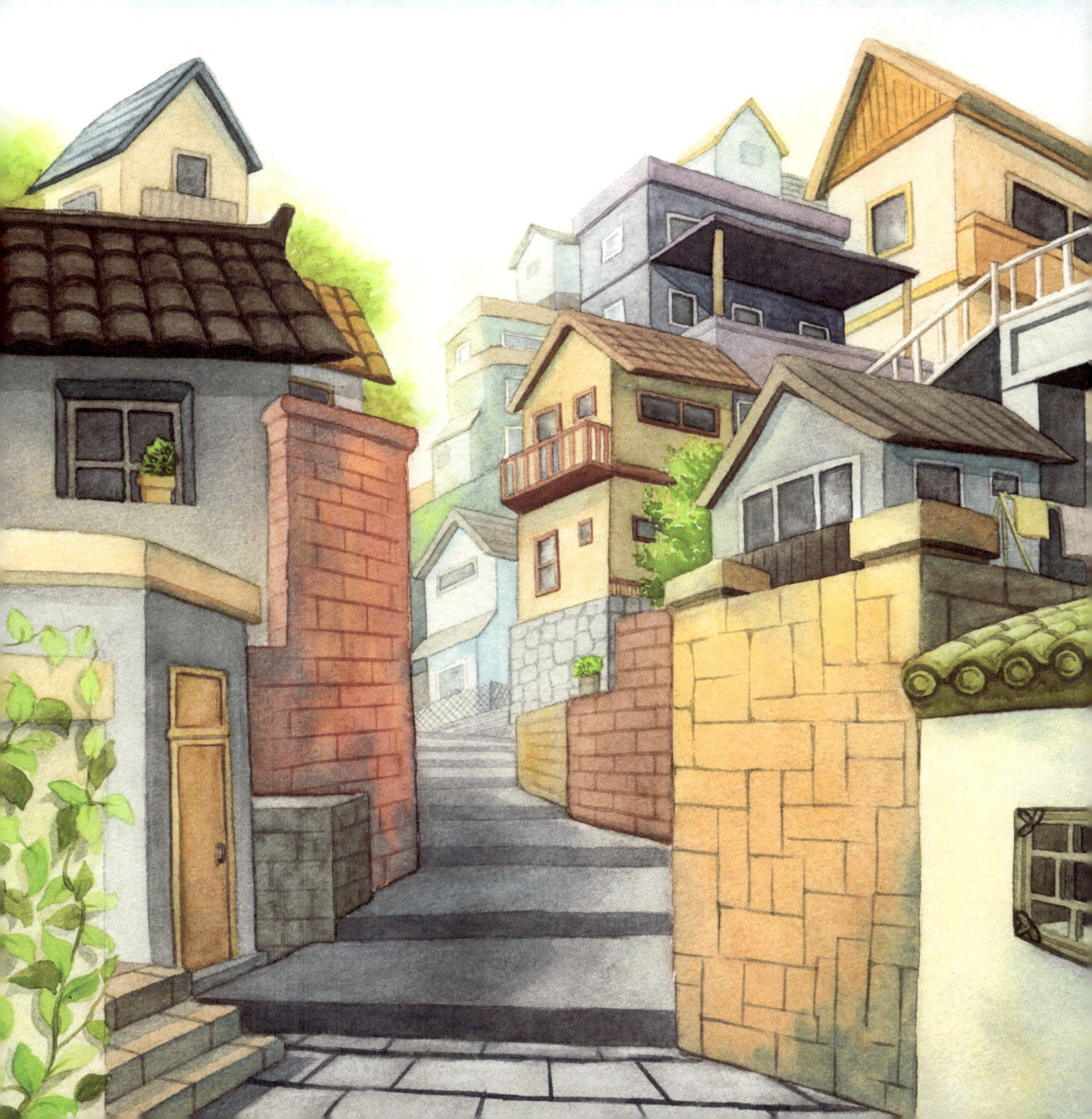

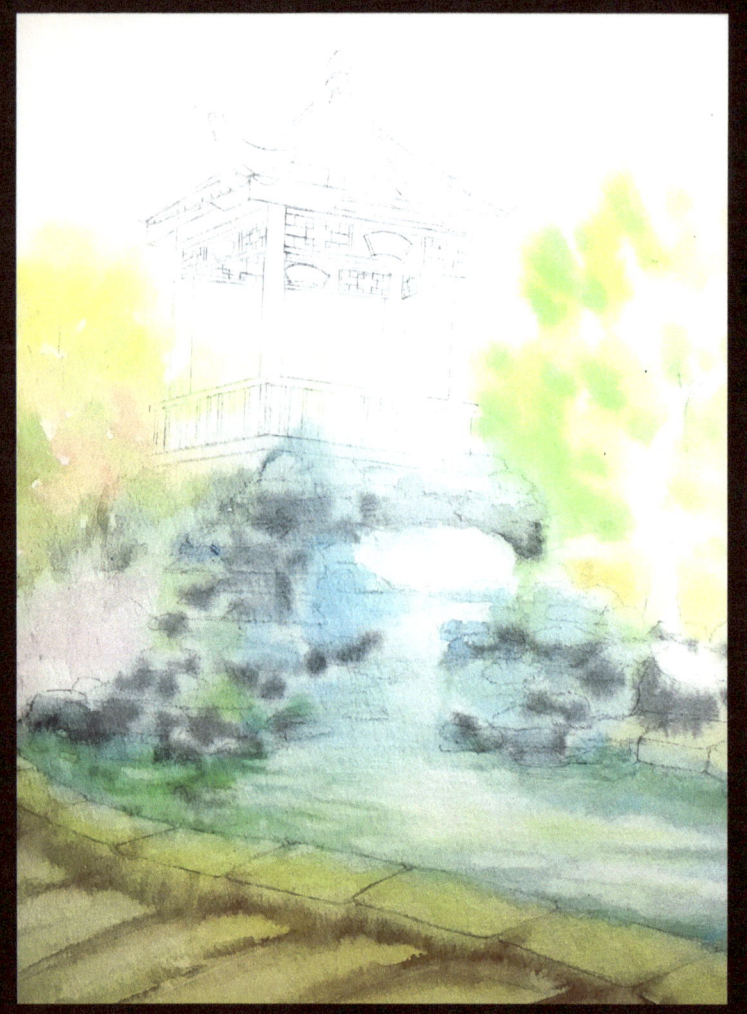
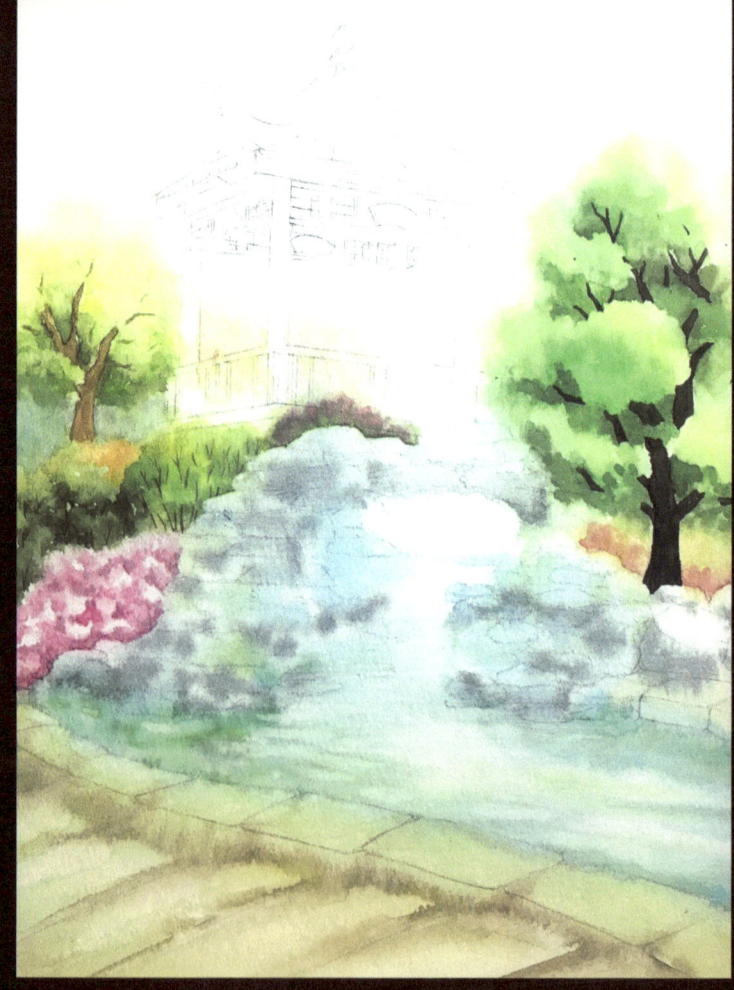

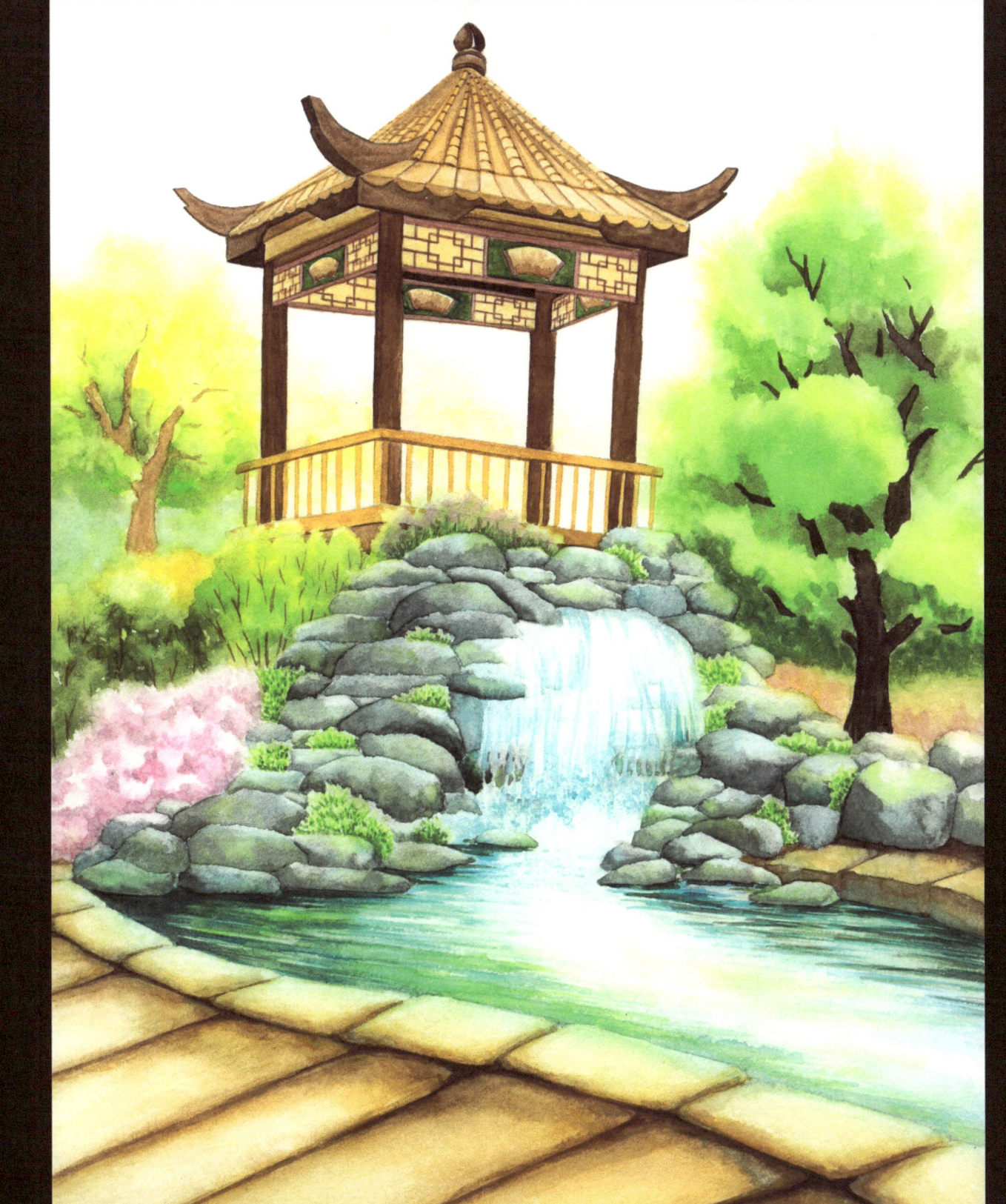

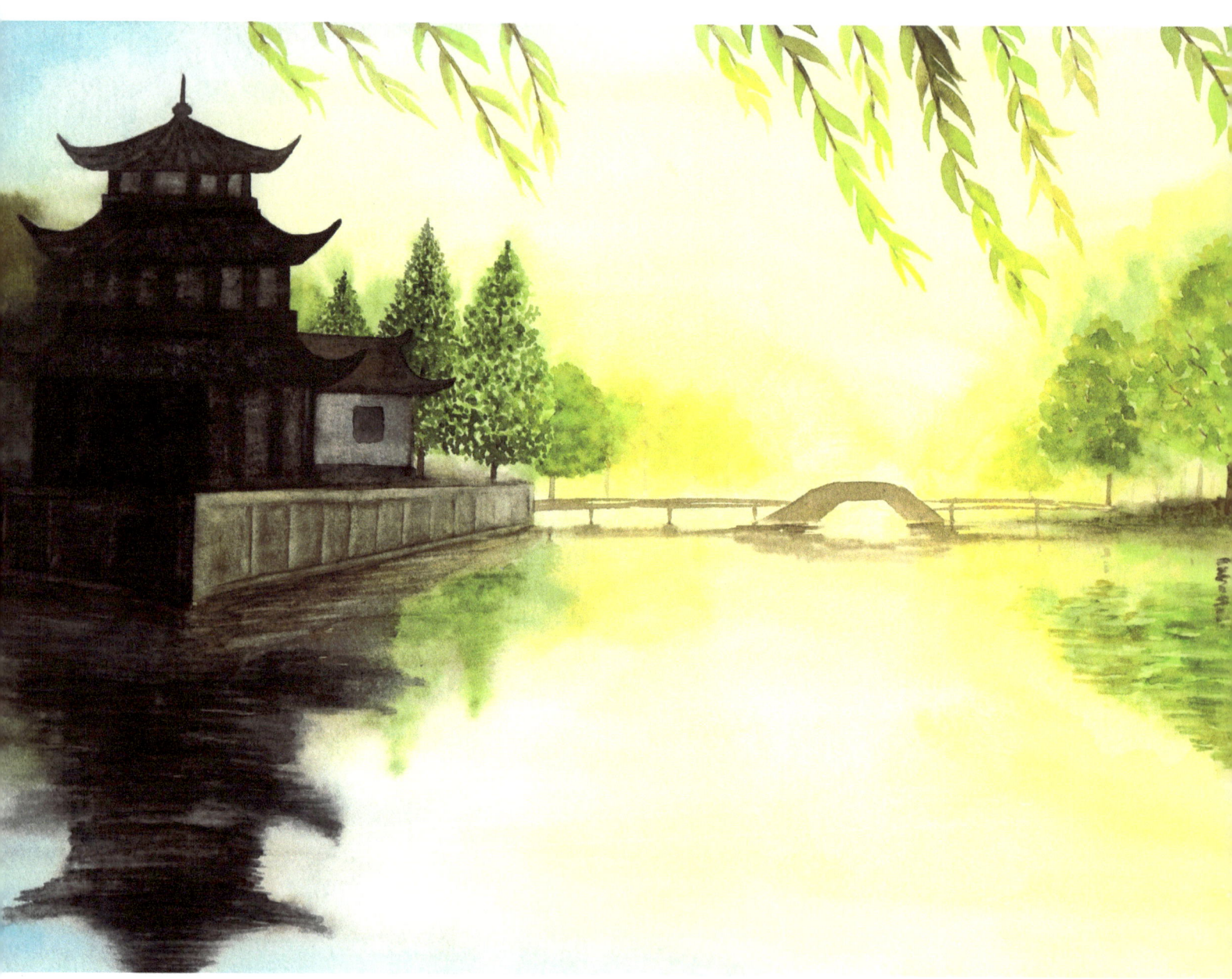

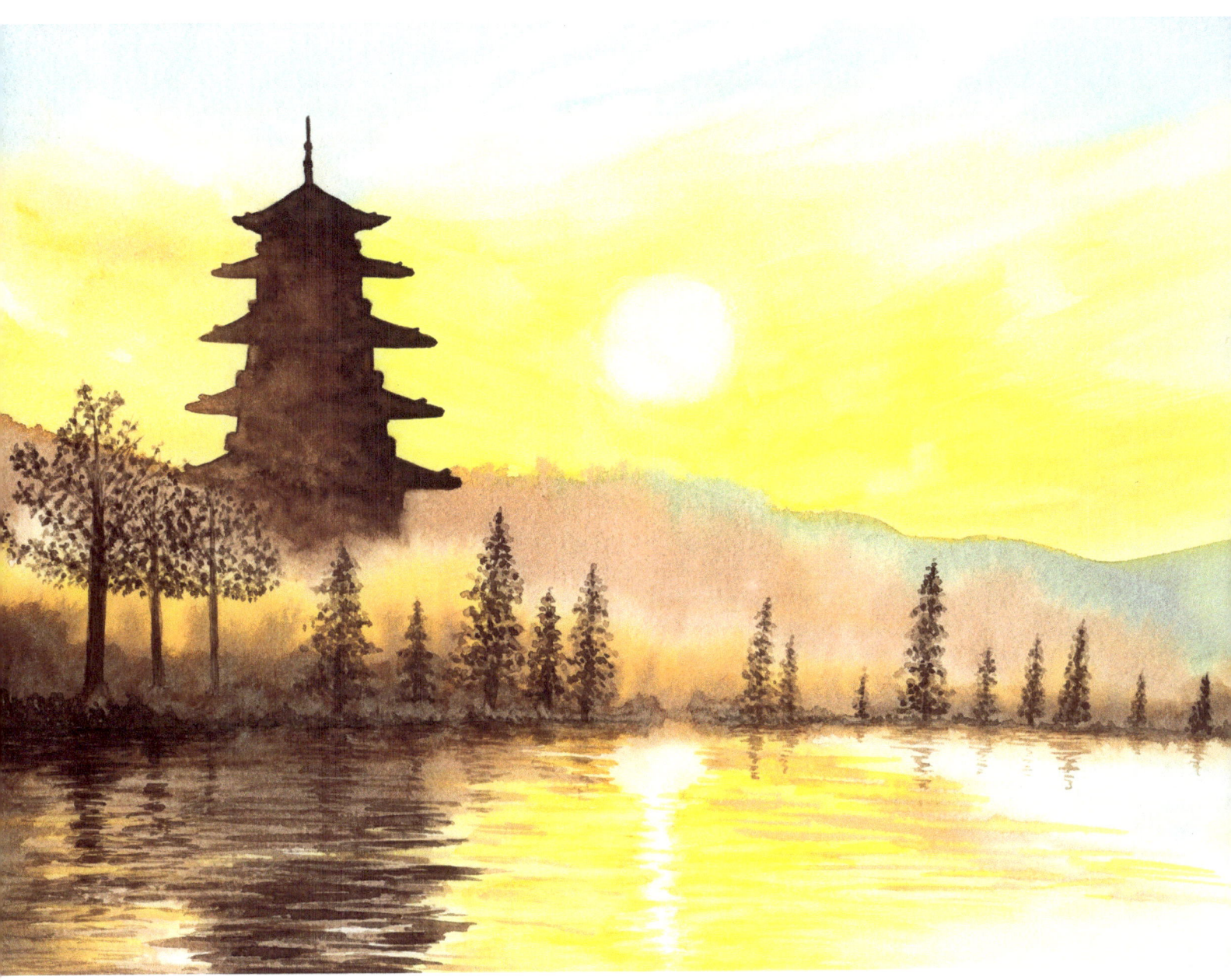

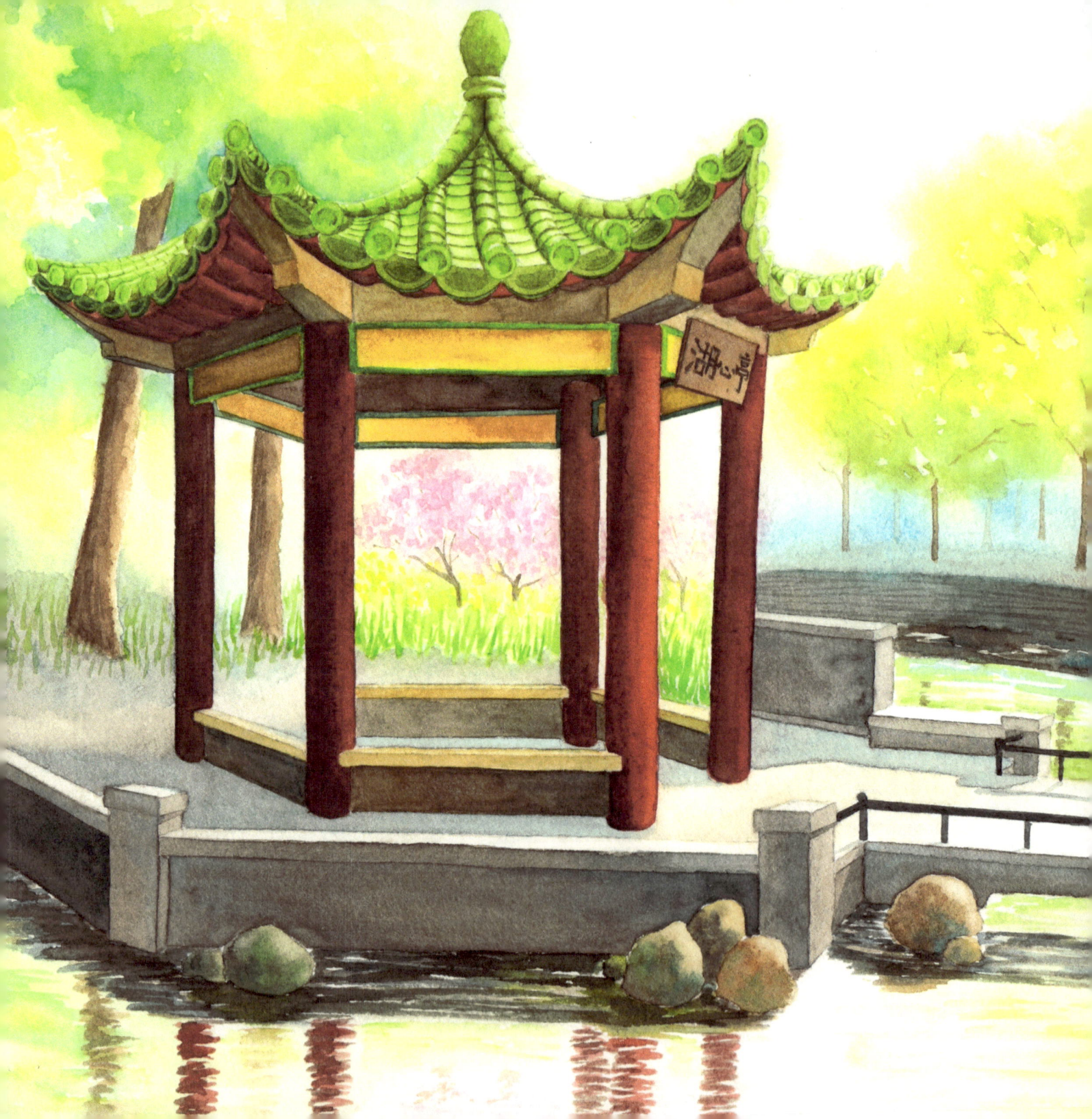

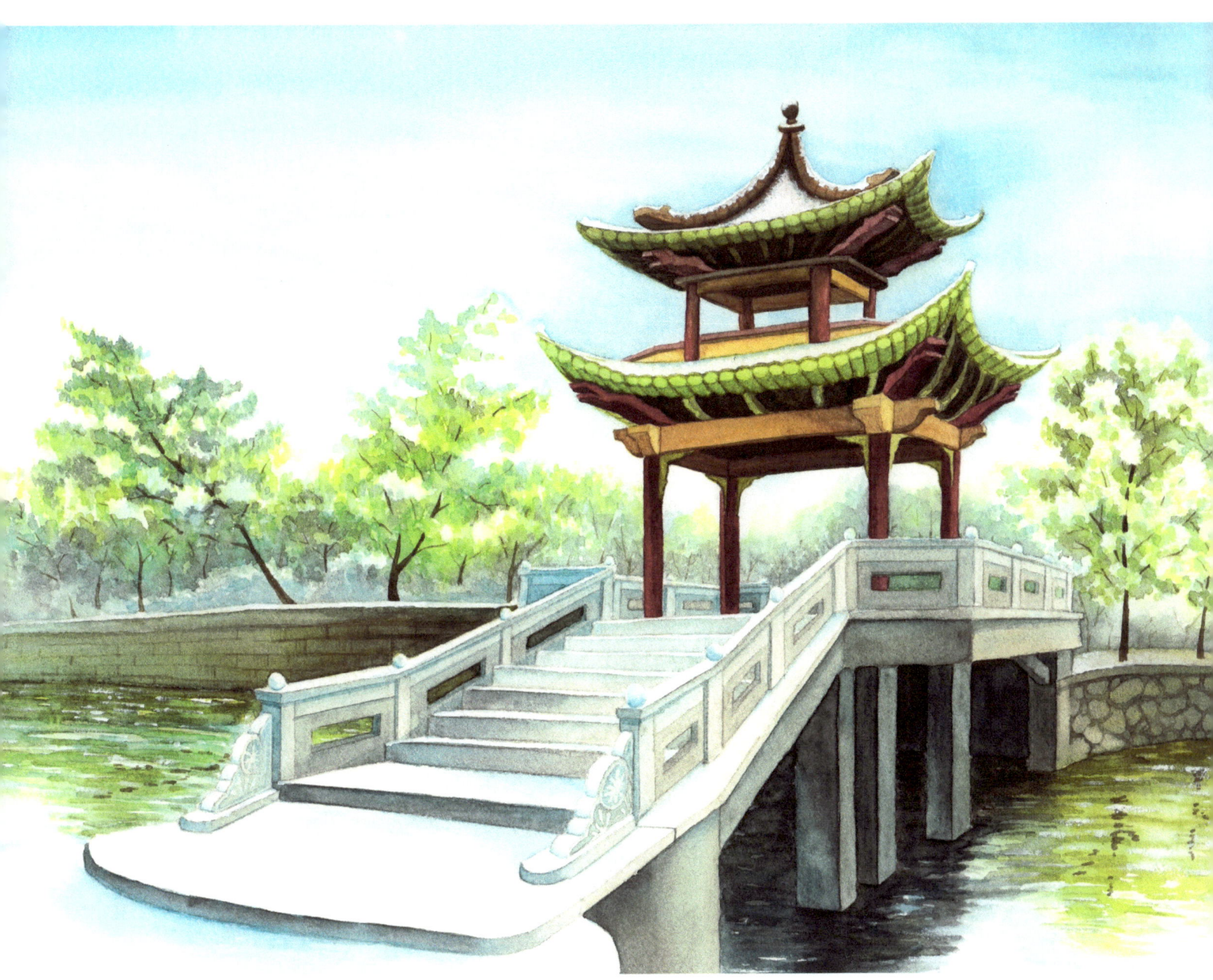

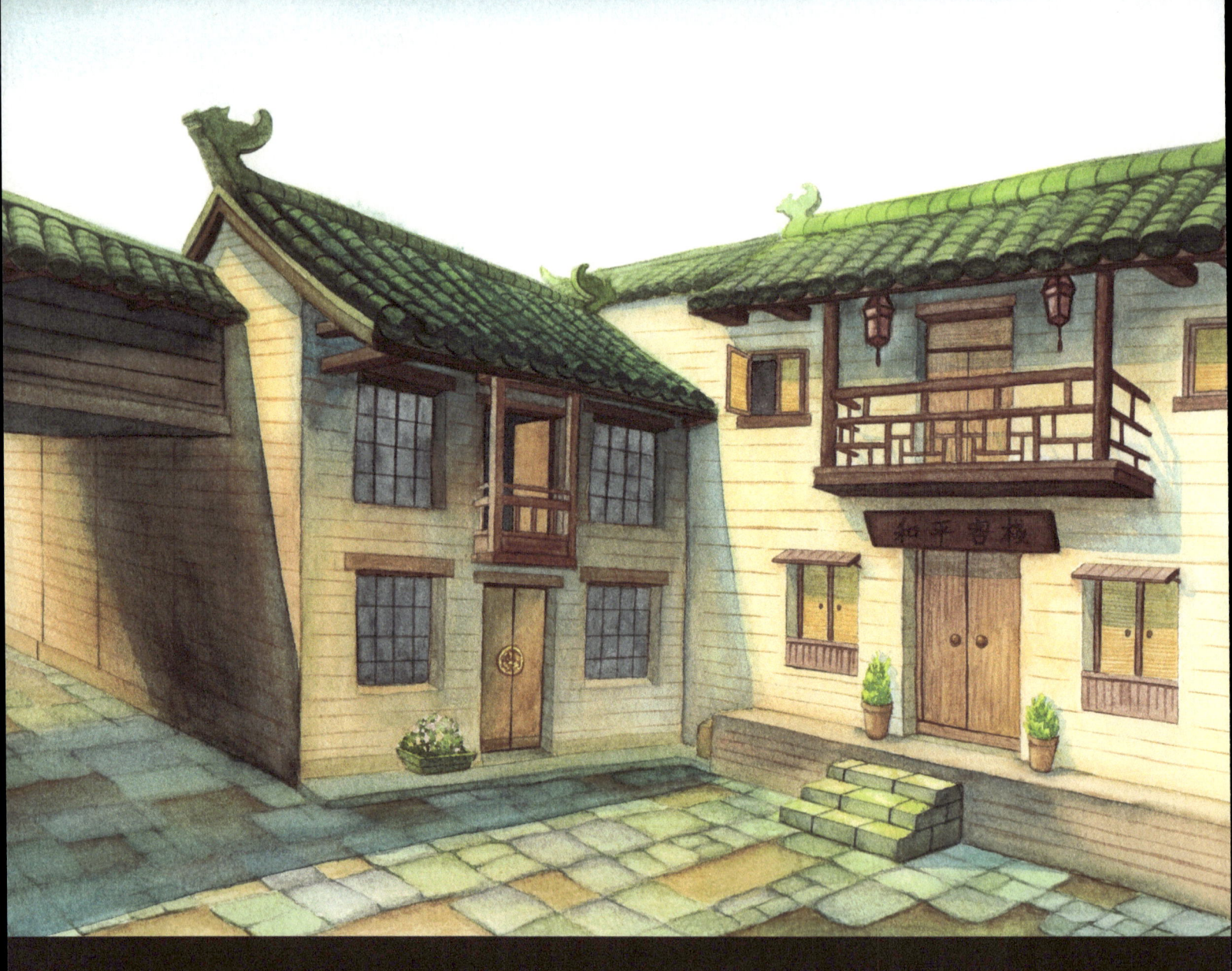

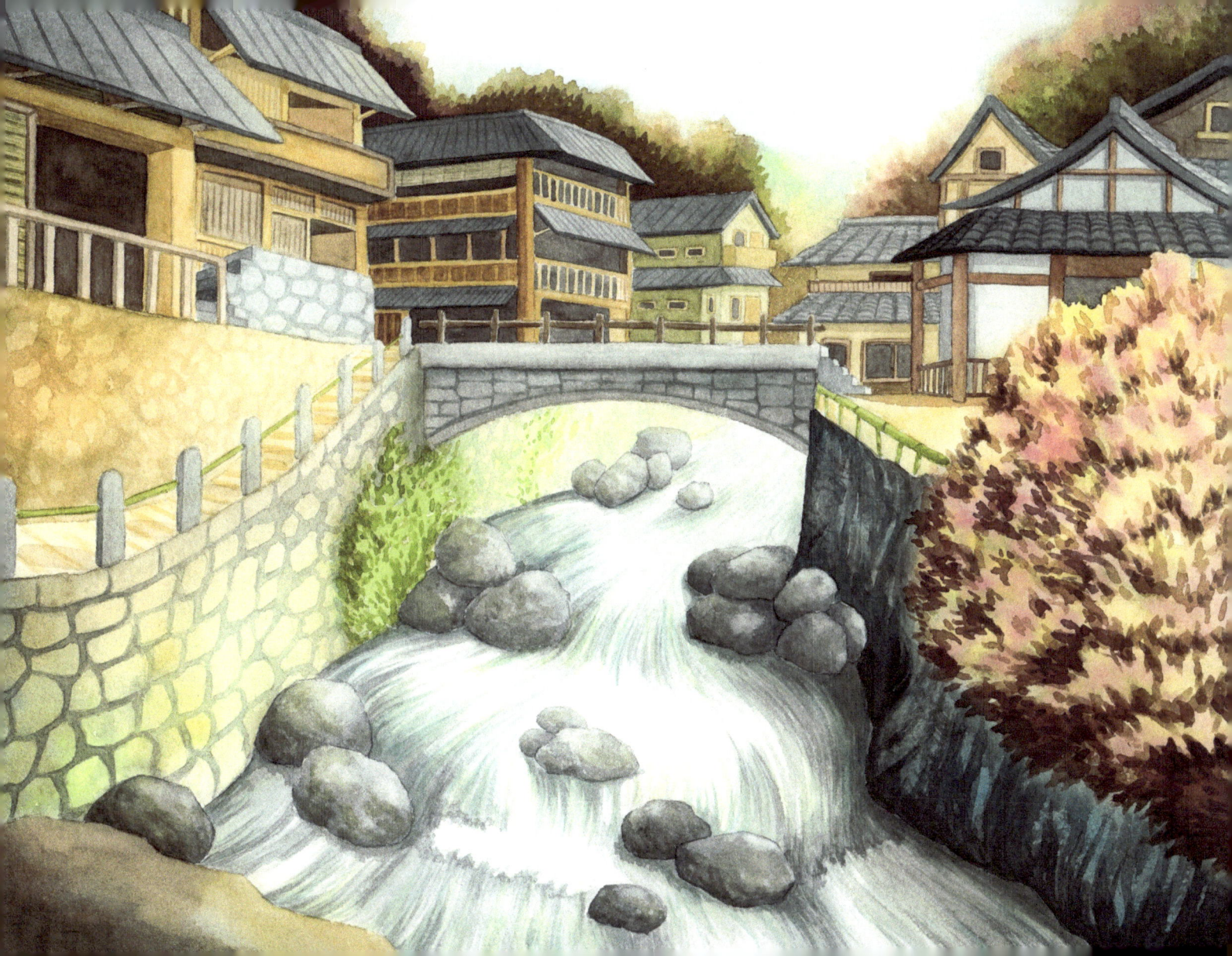

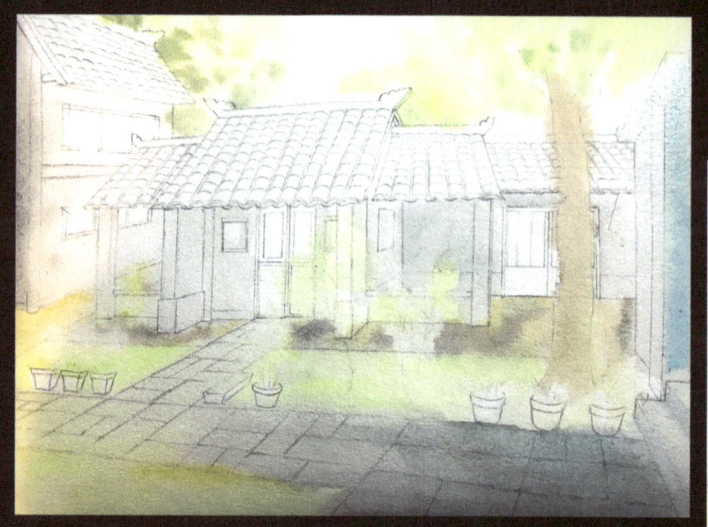

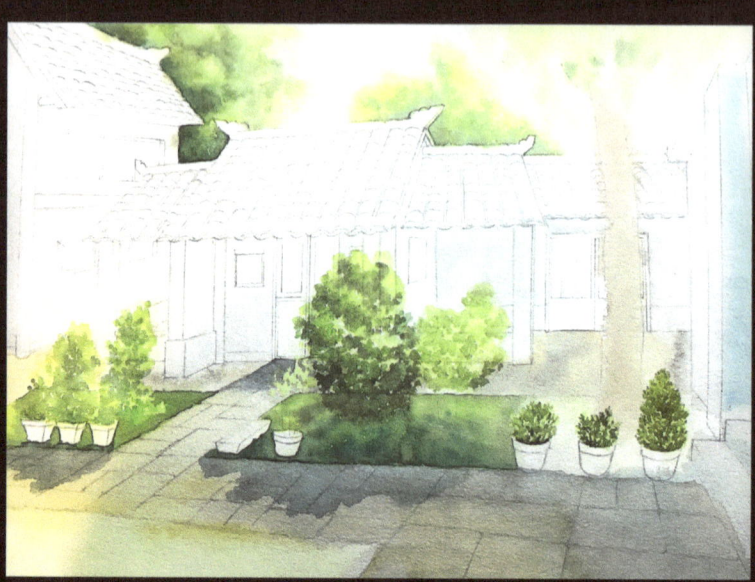

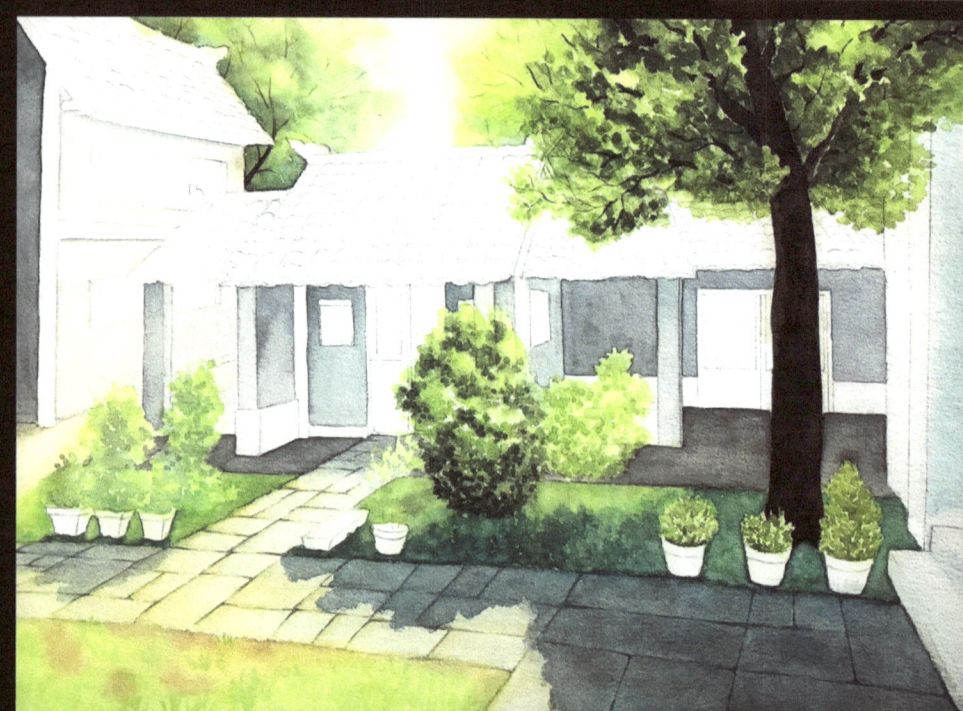

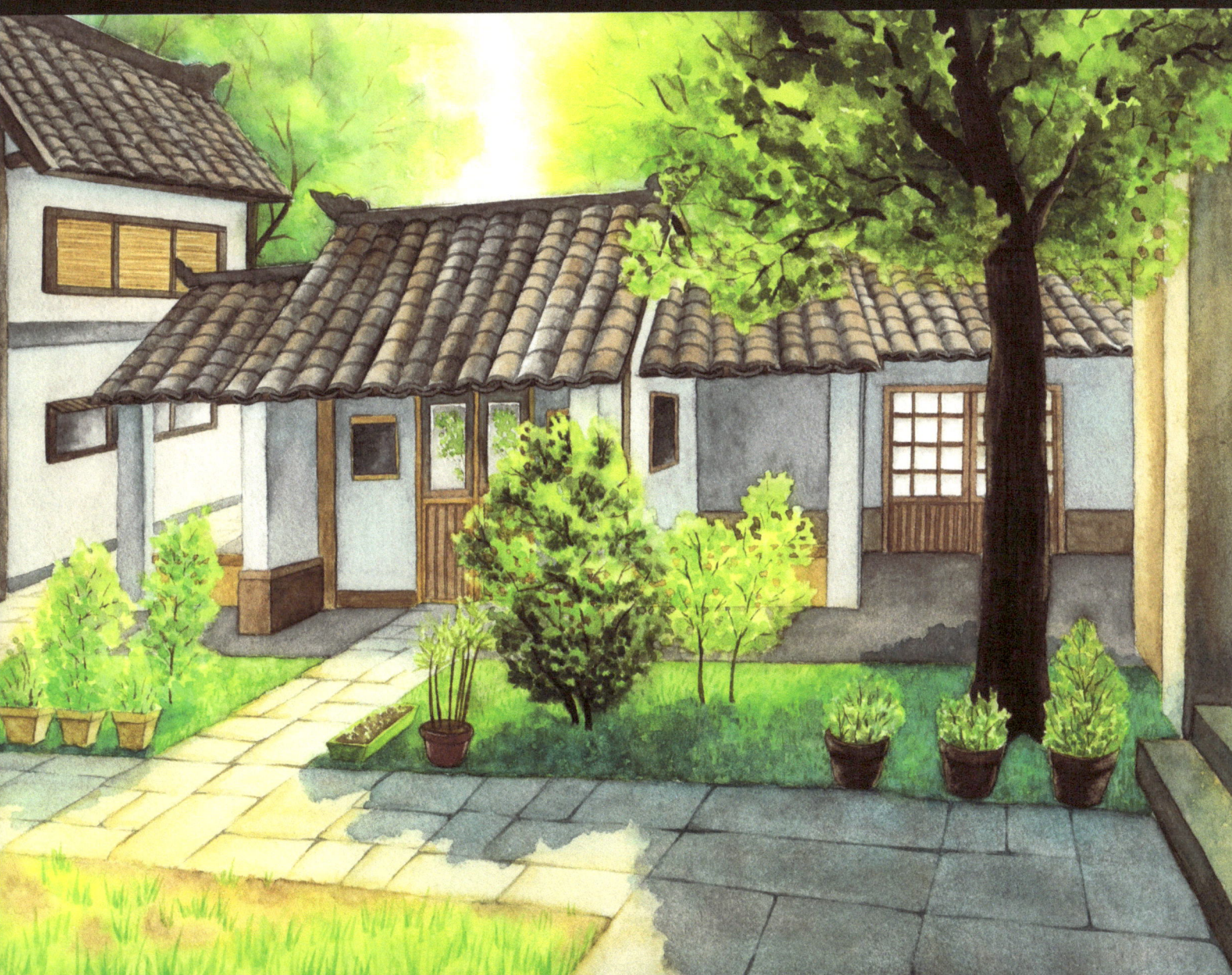

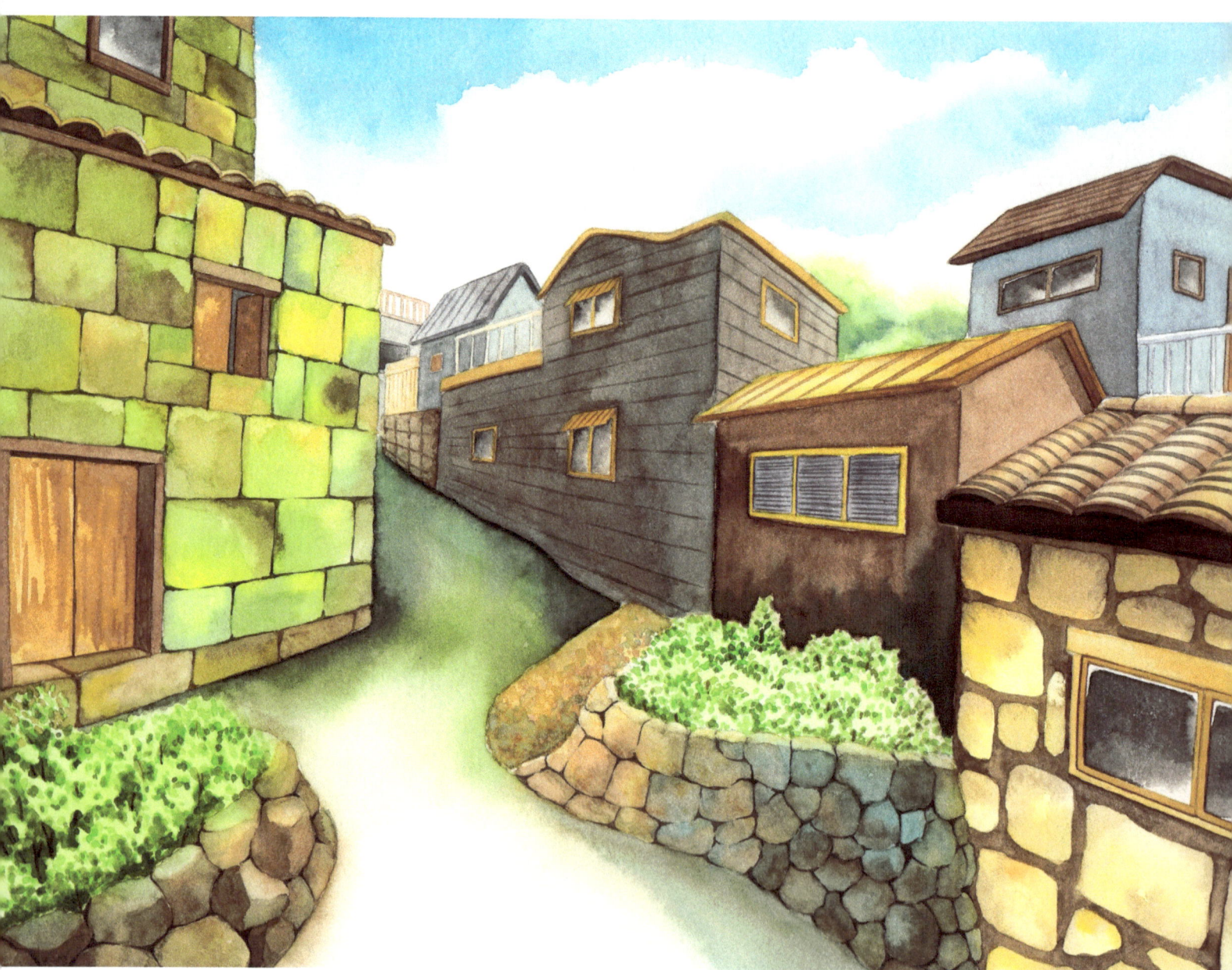

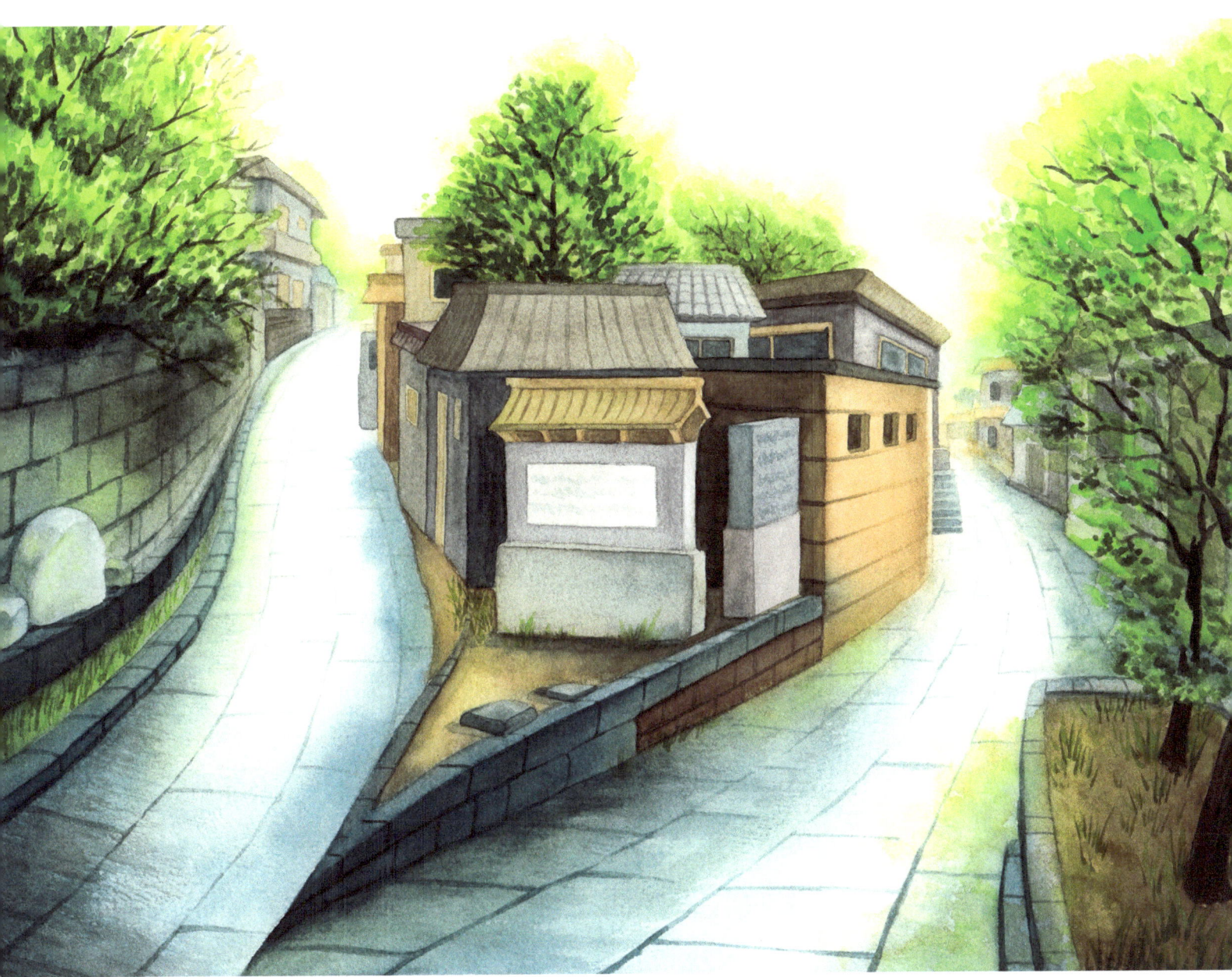

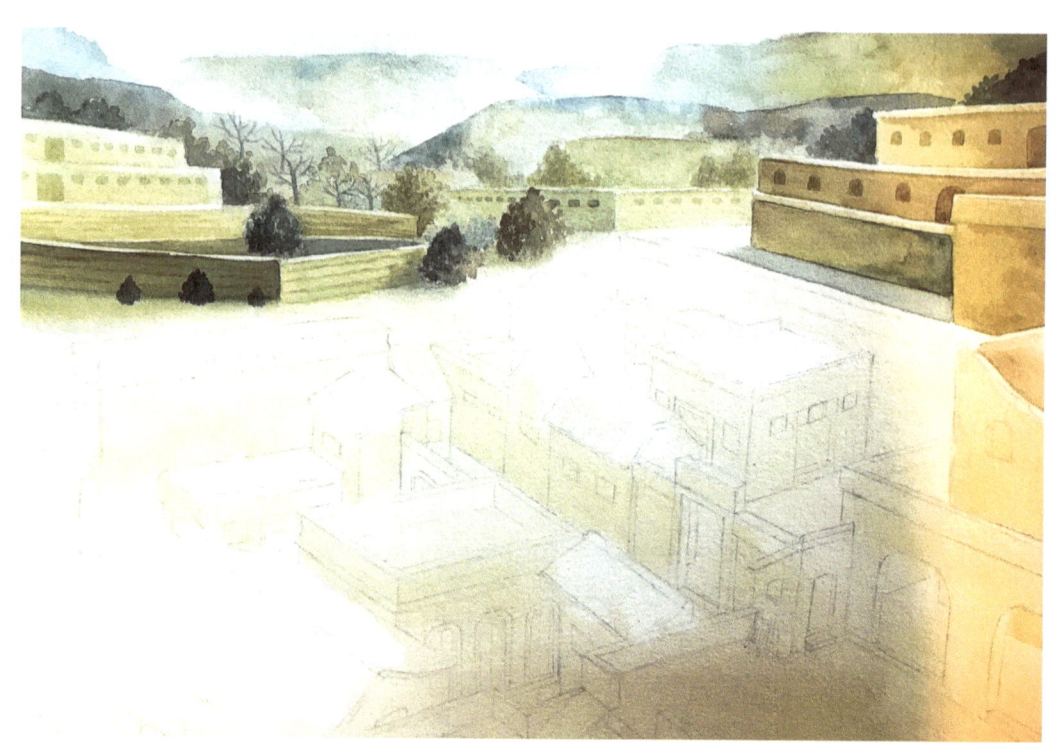

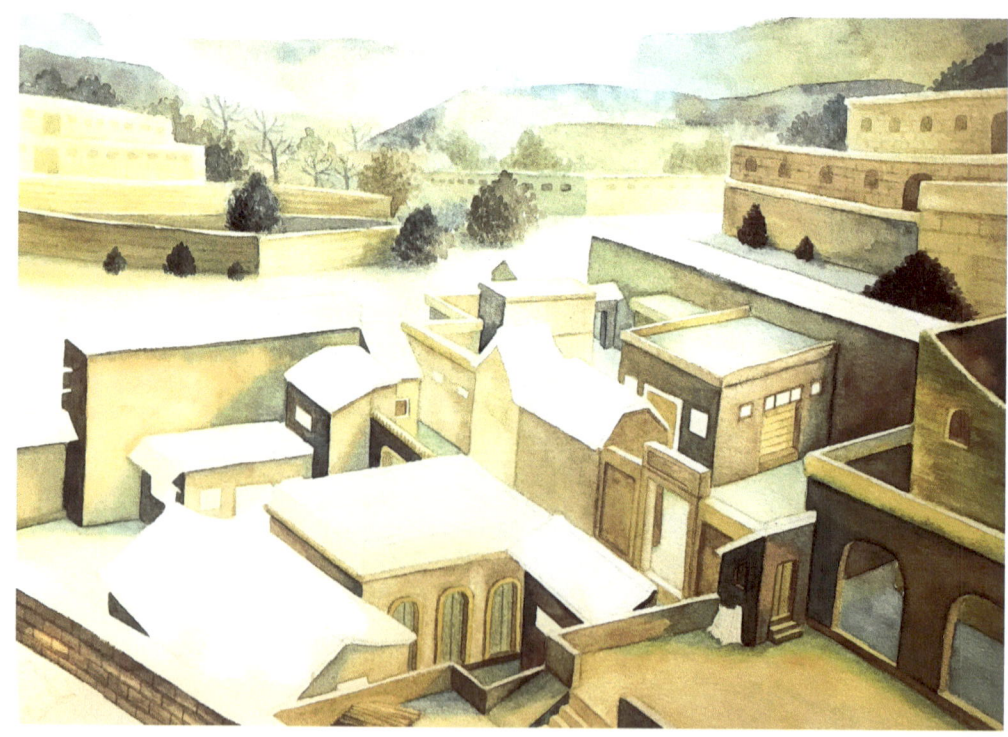

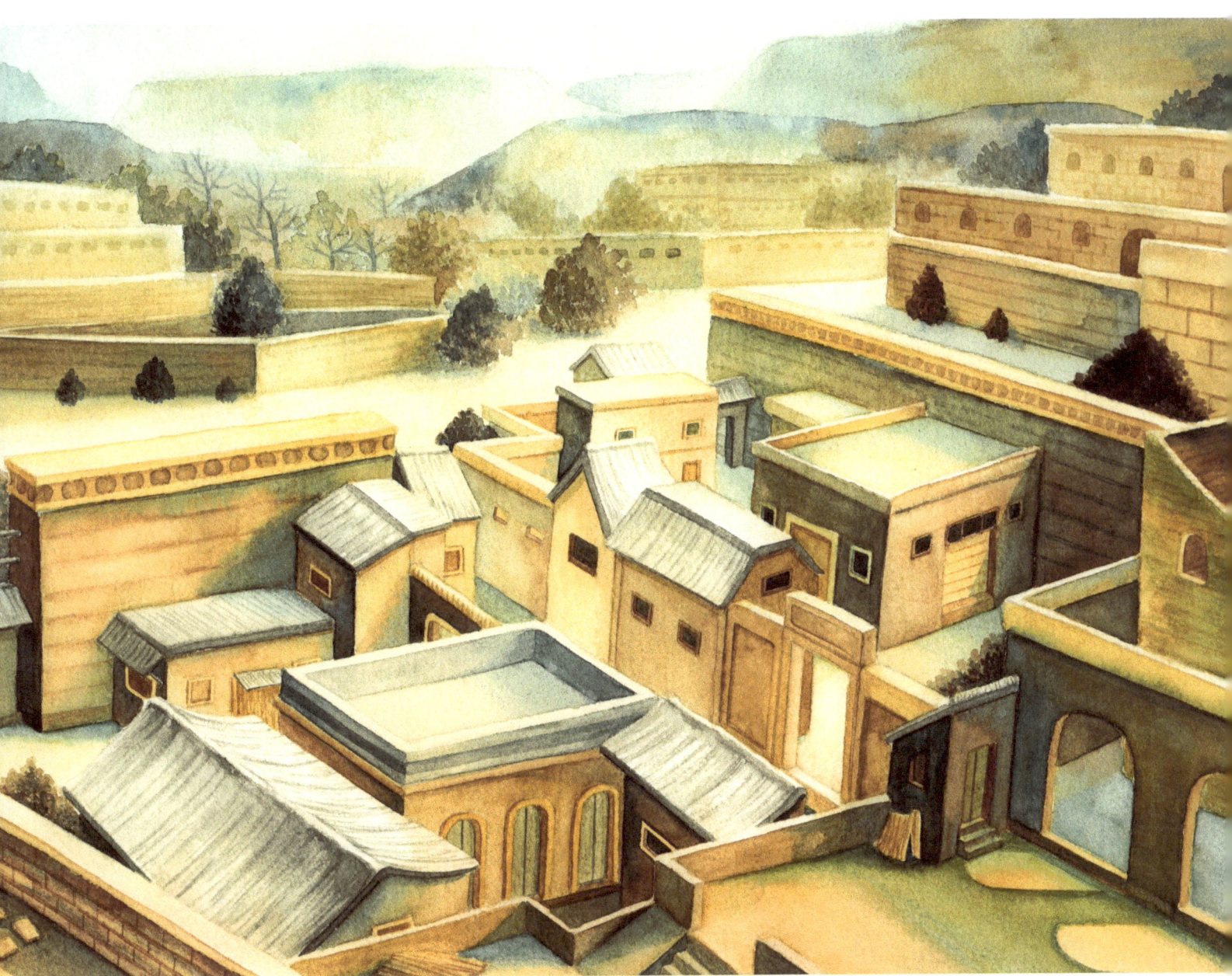

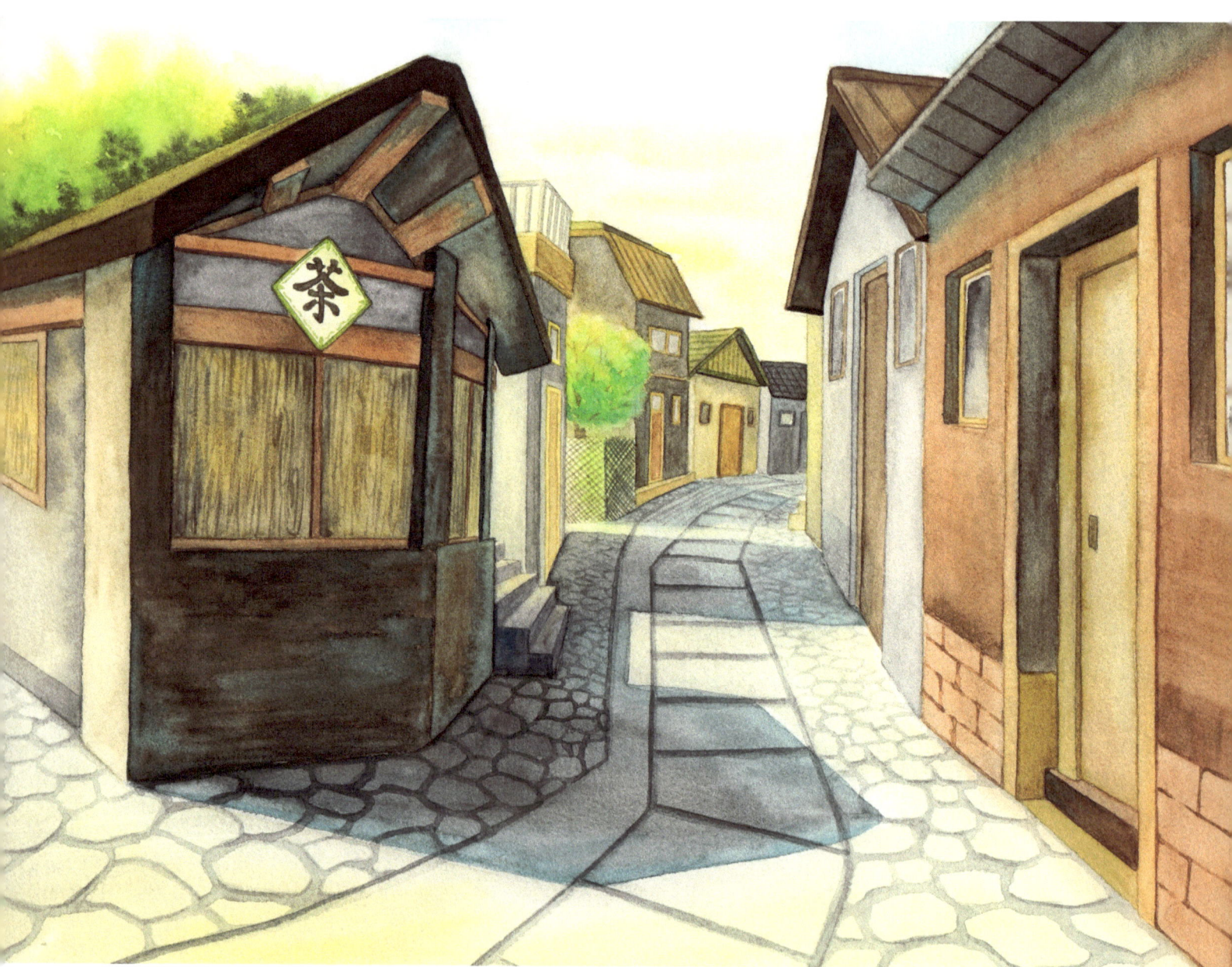

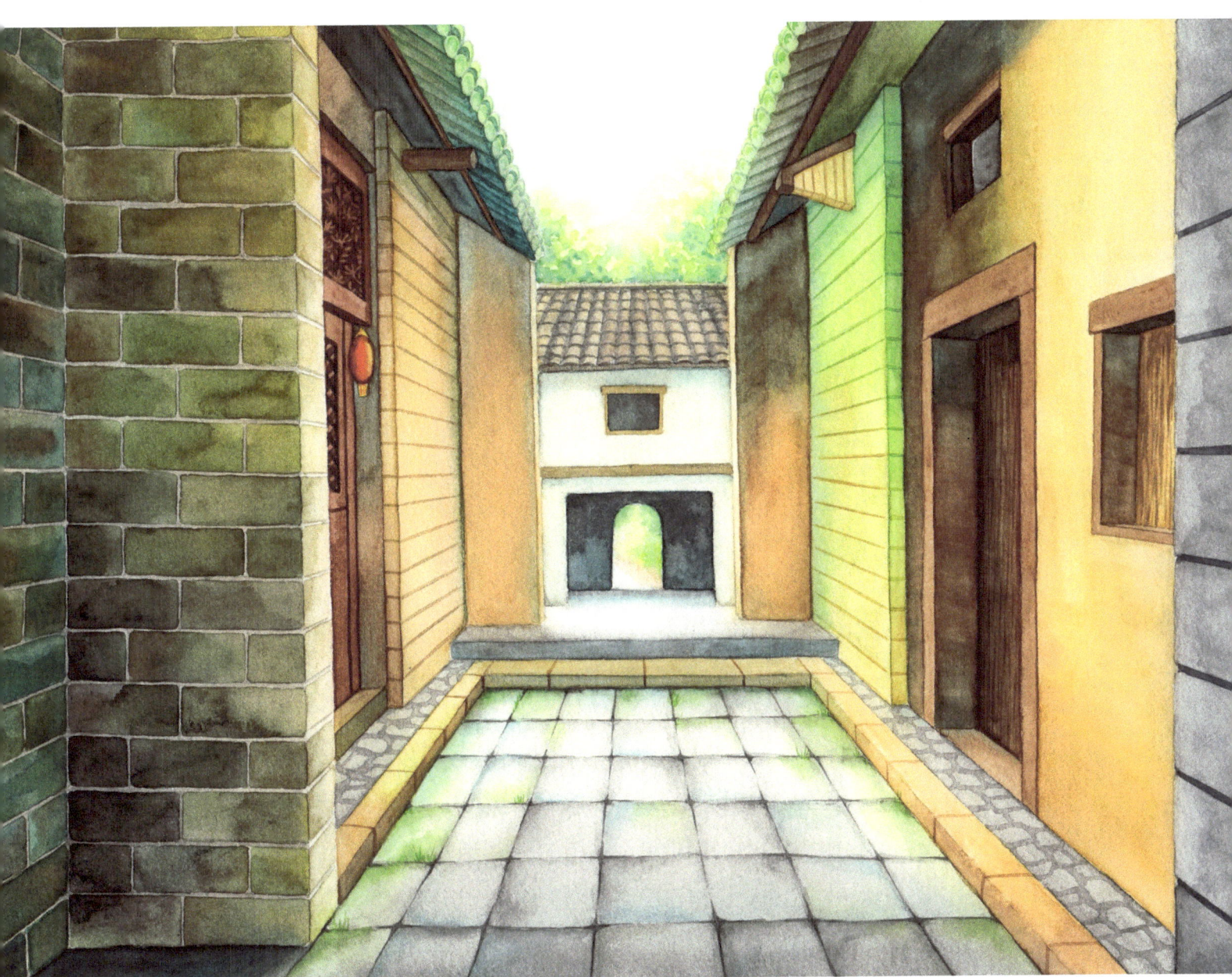

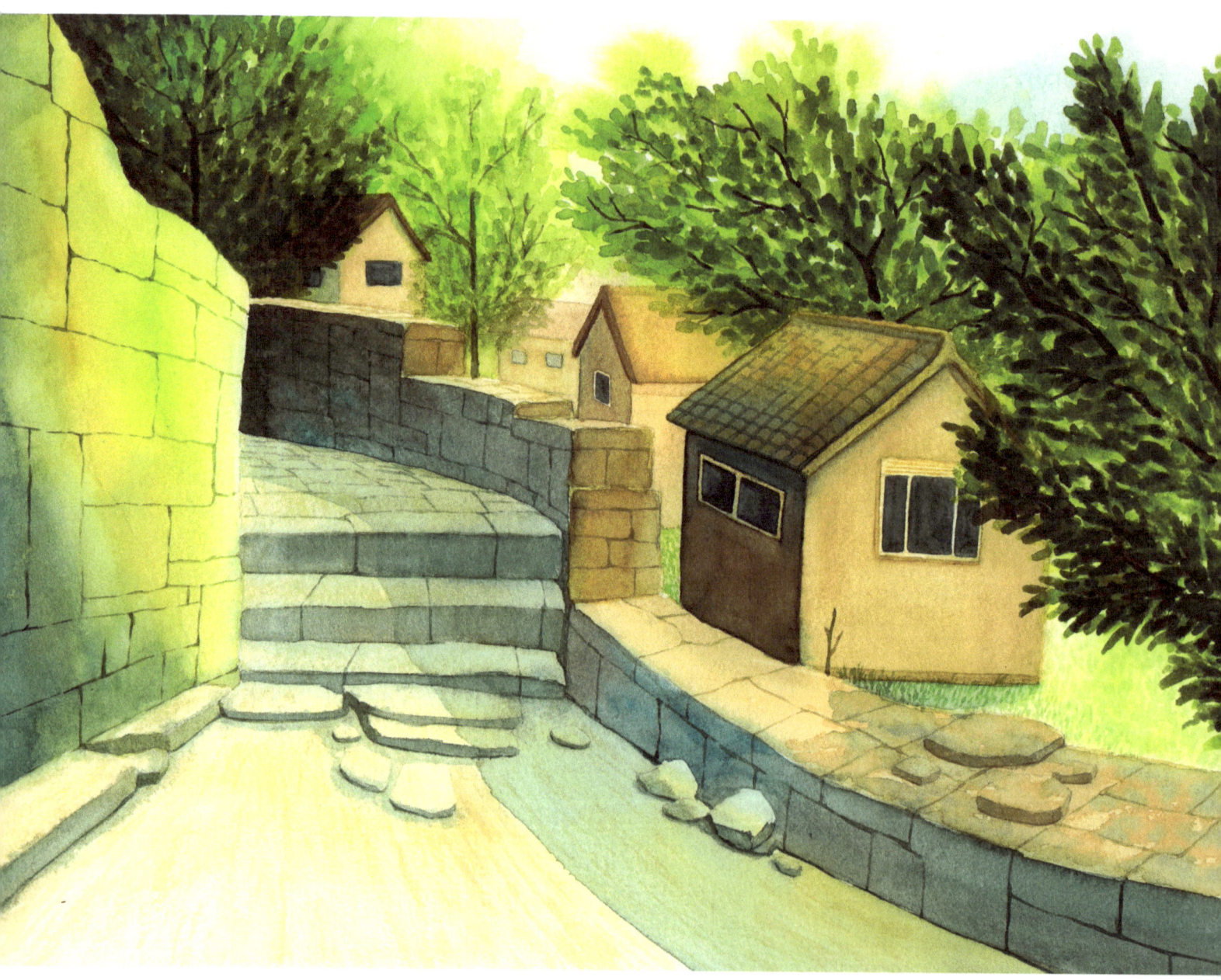

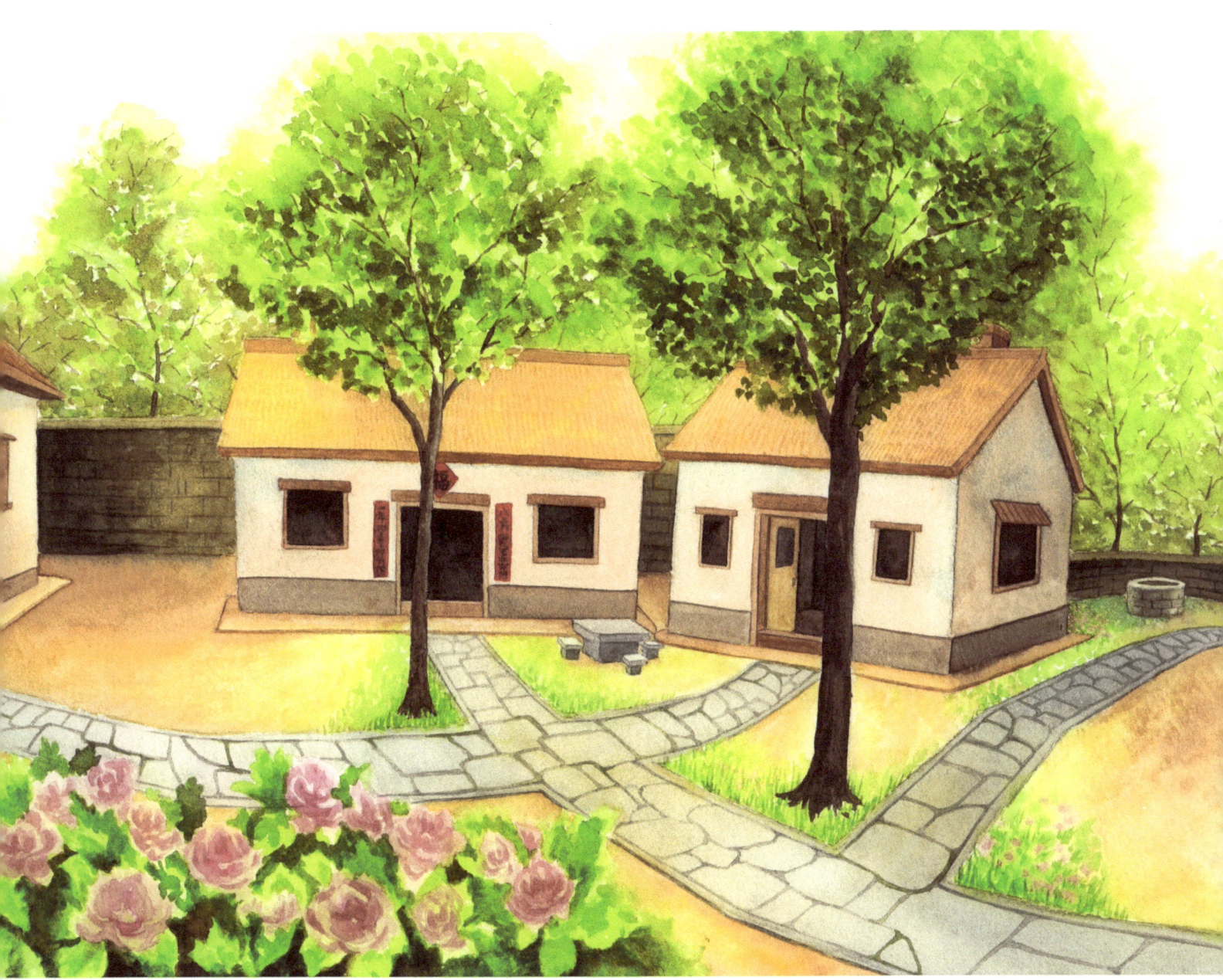

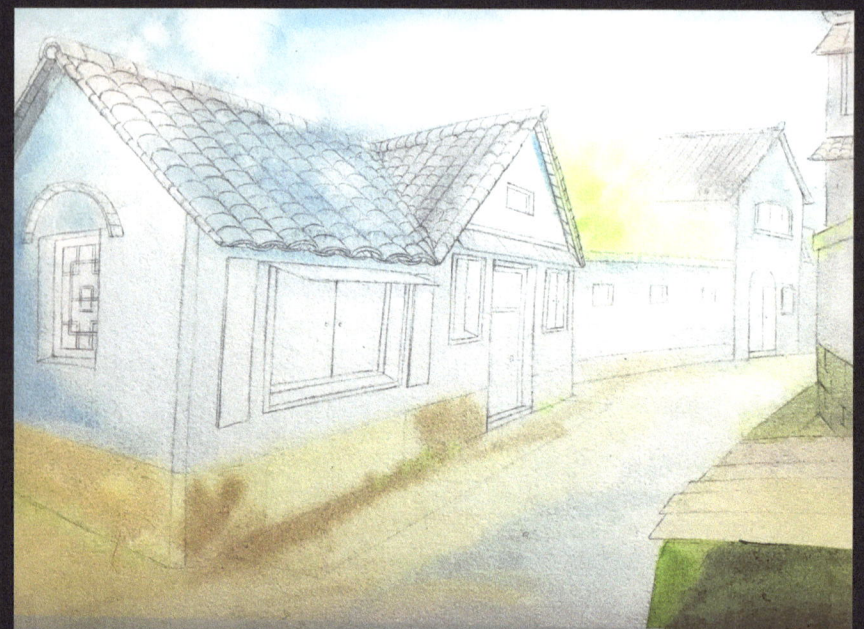
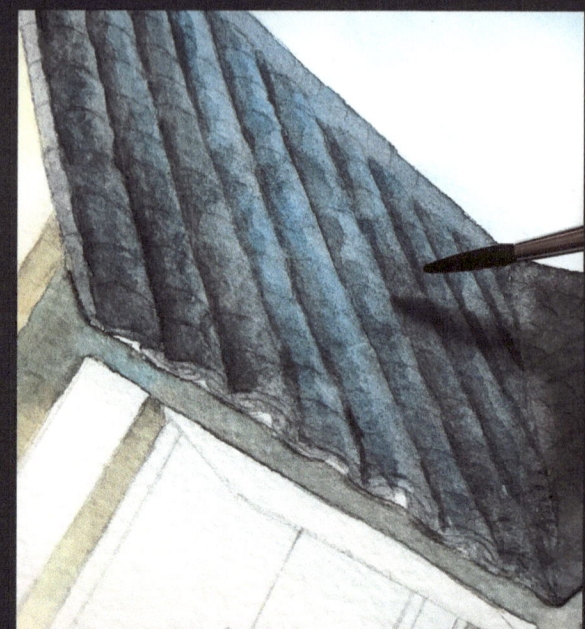

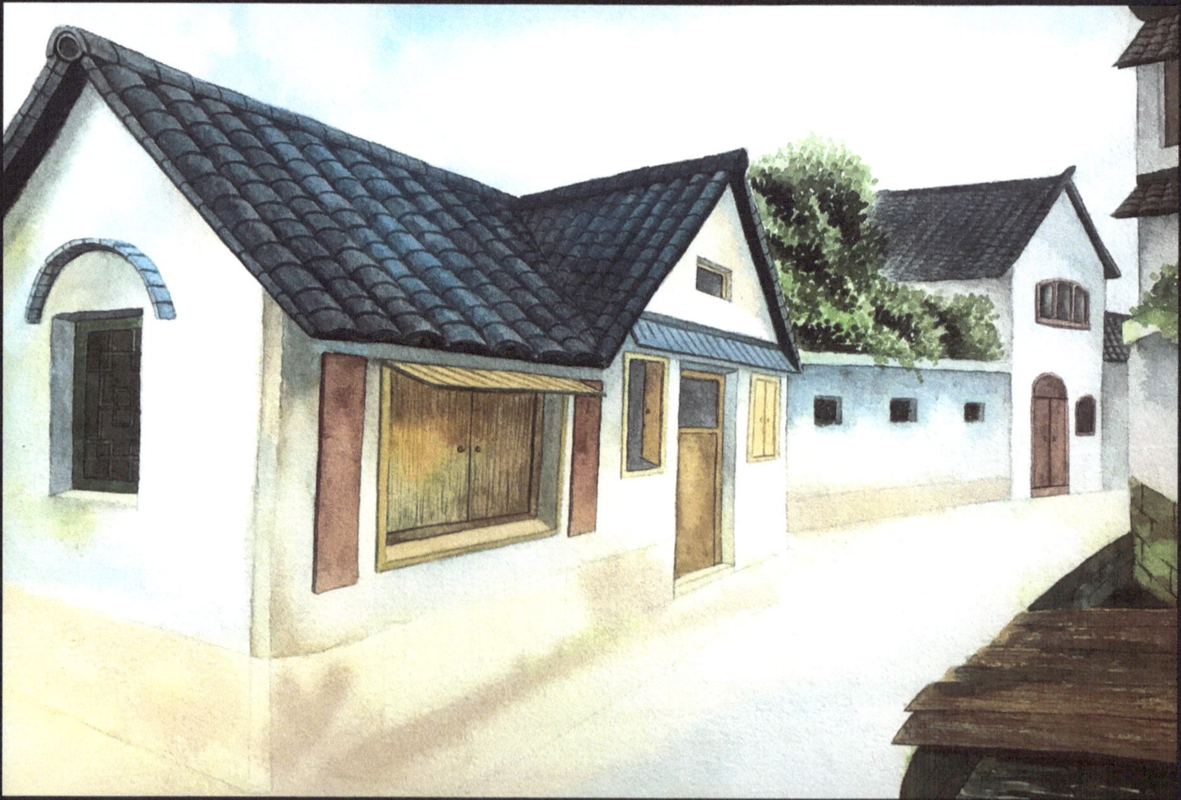

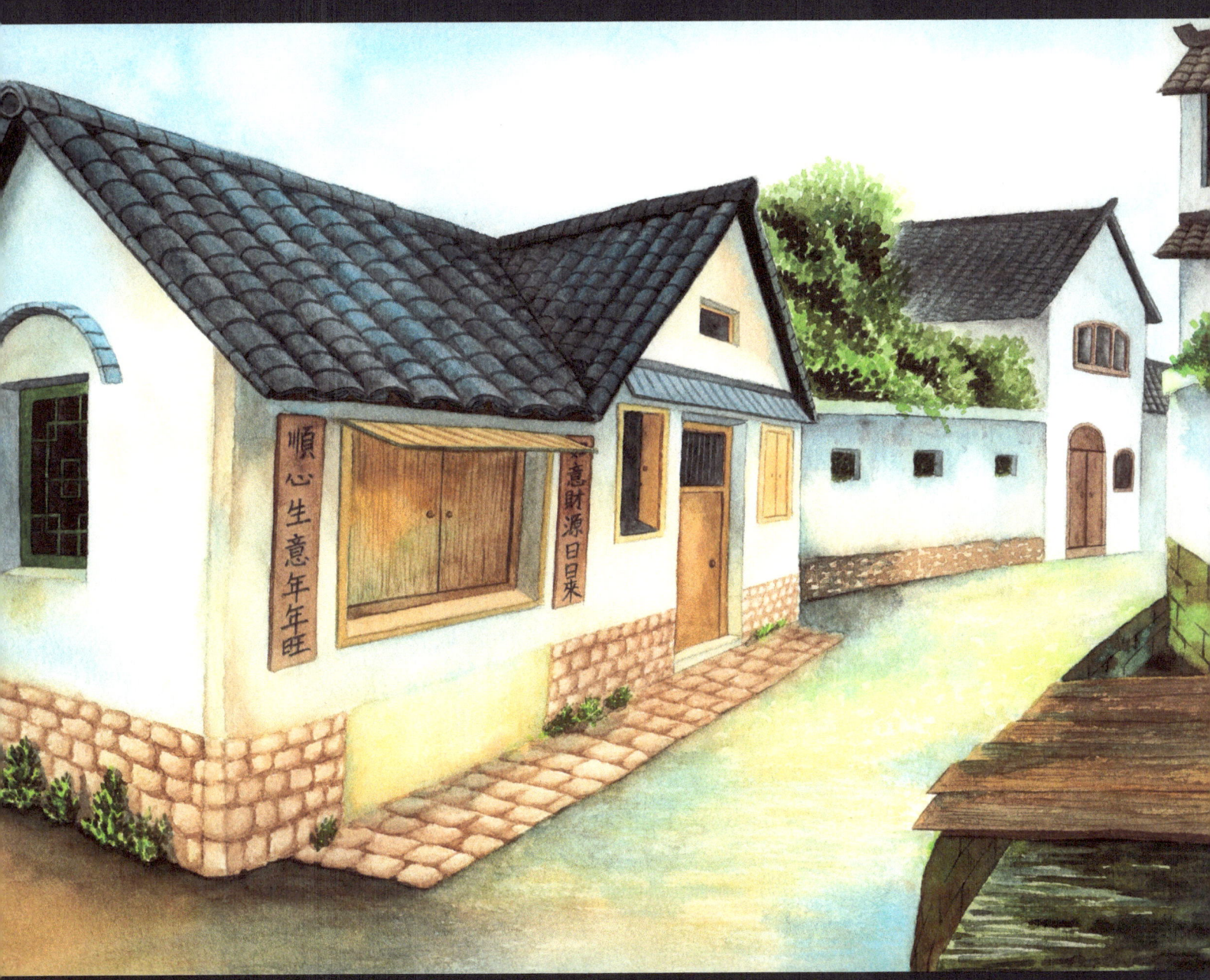

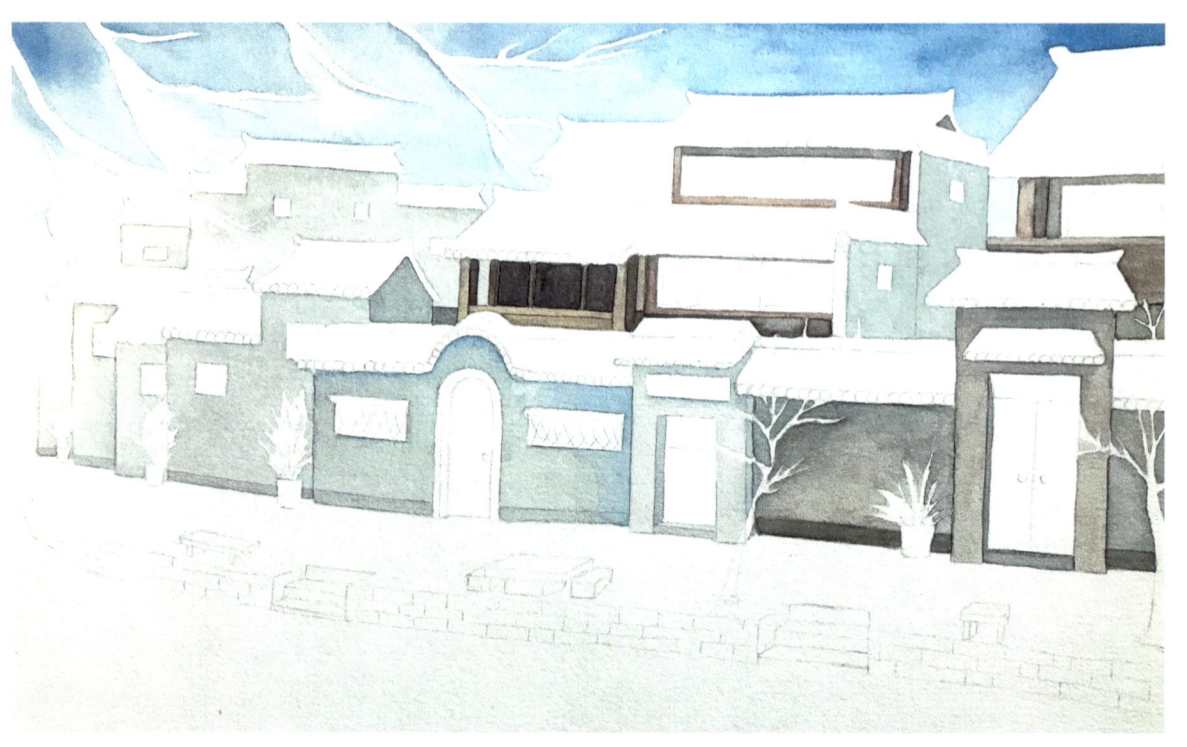

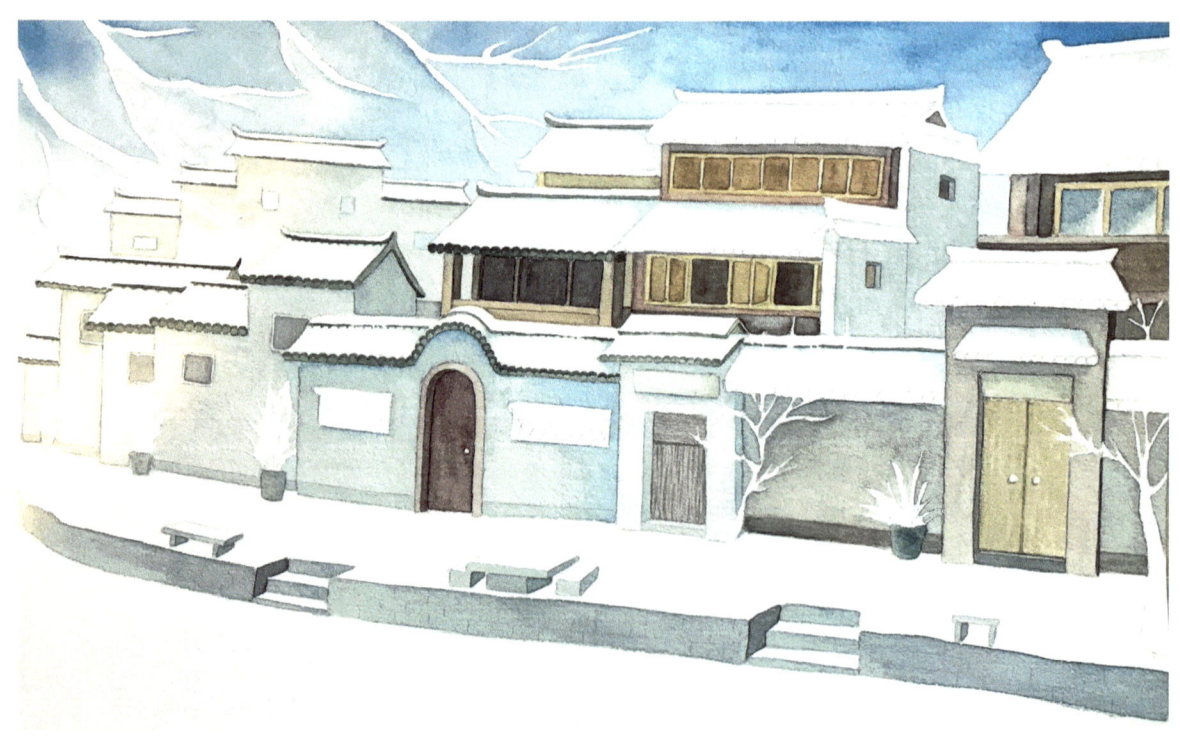

72

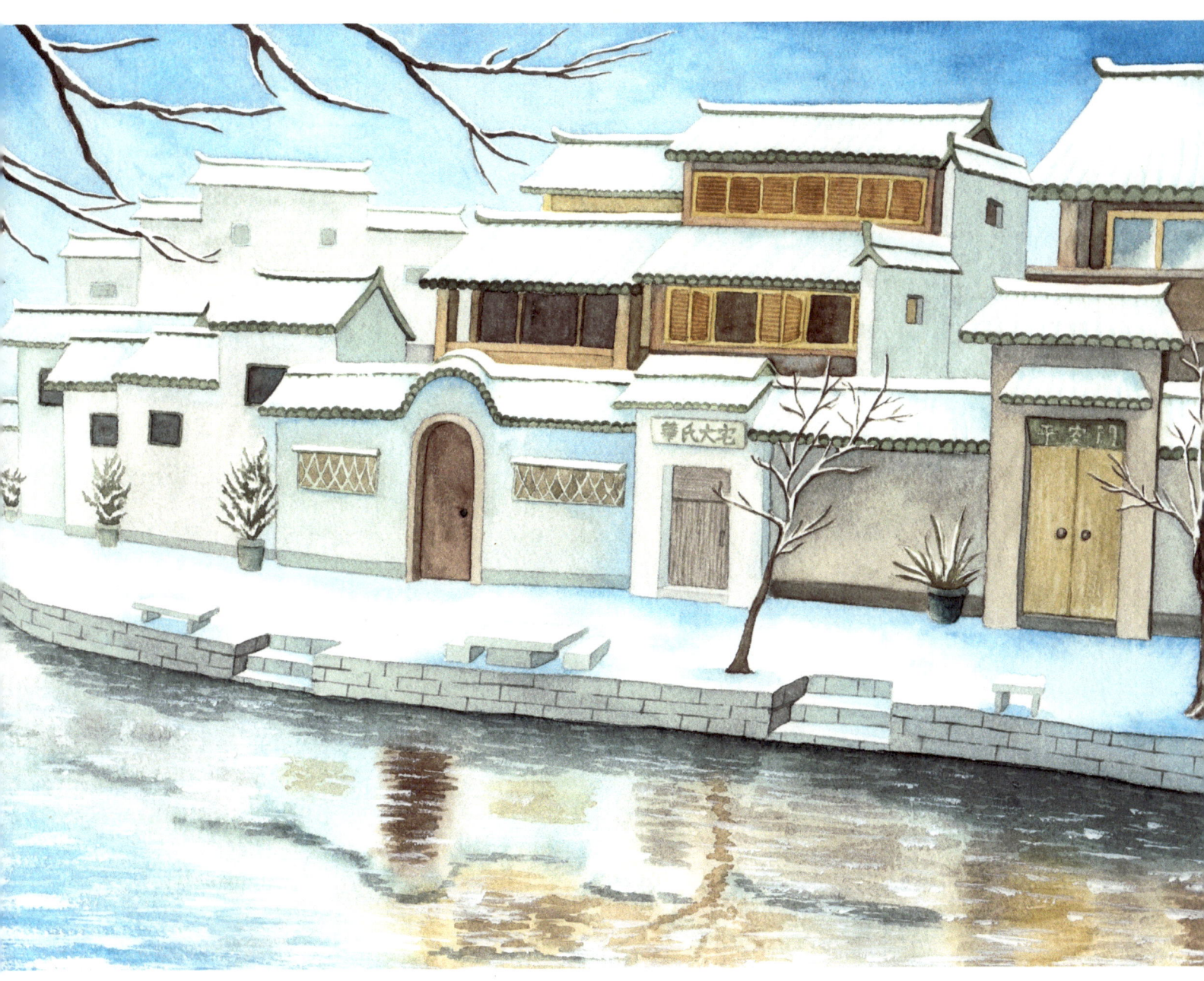

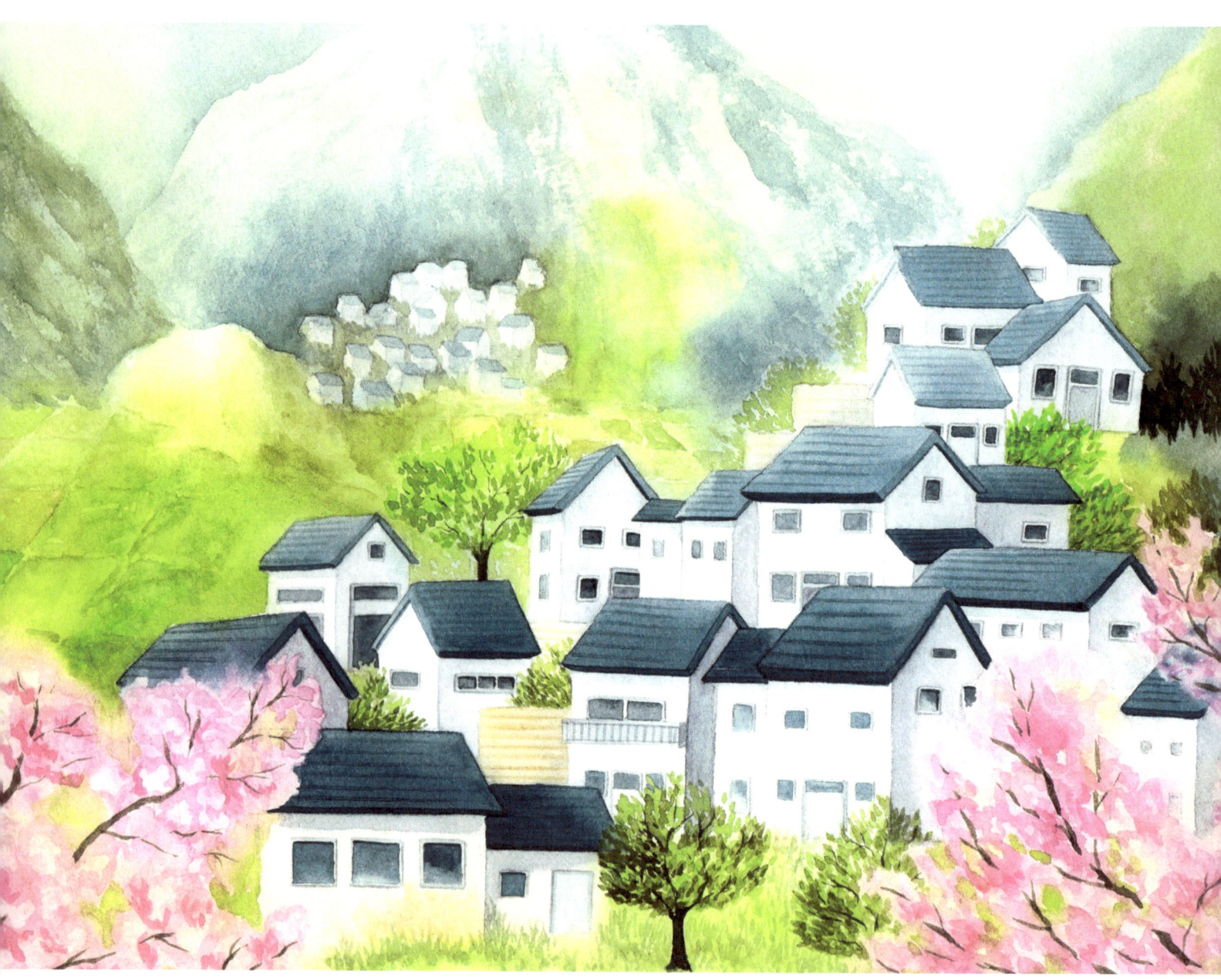

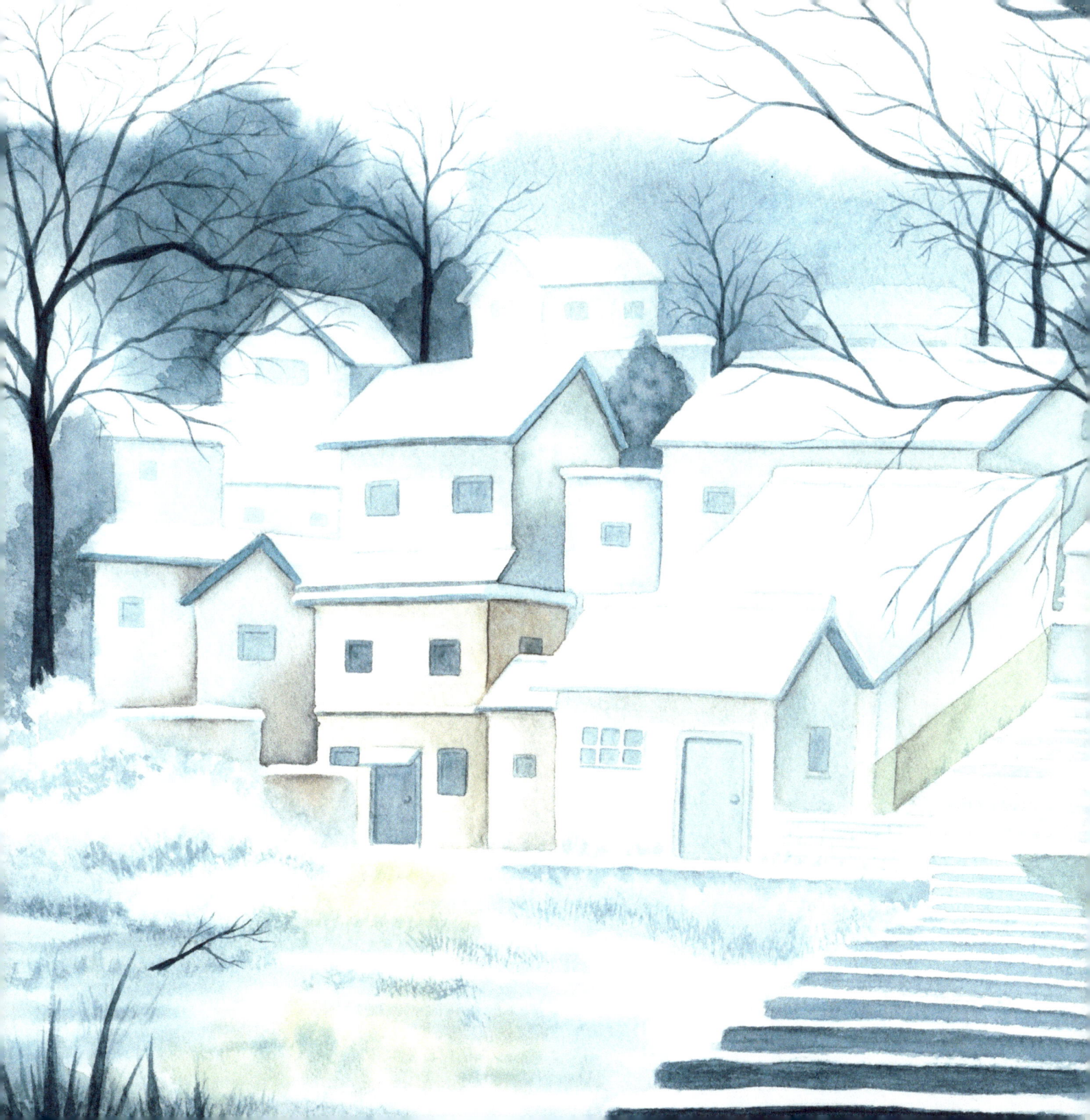

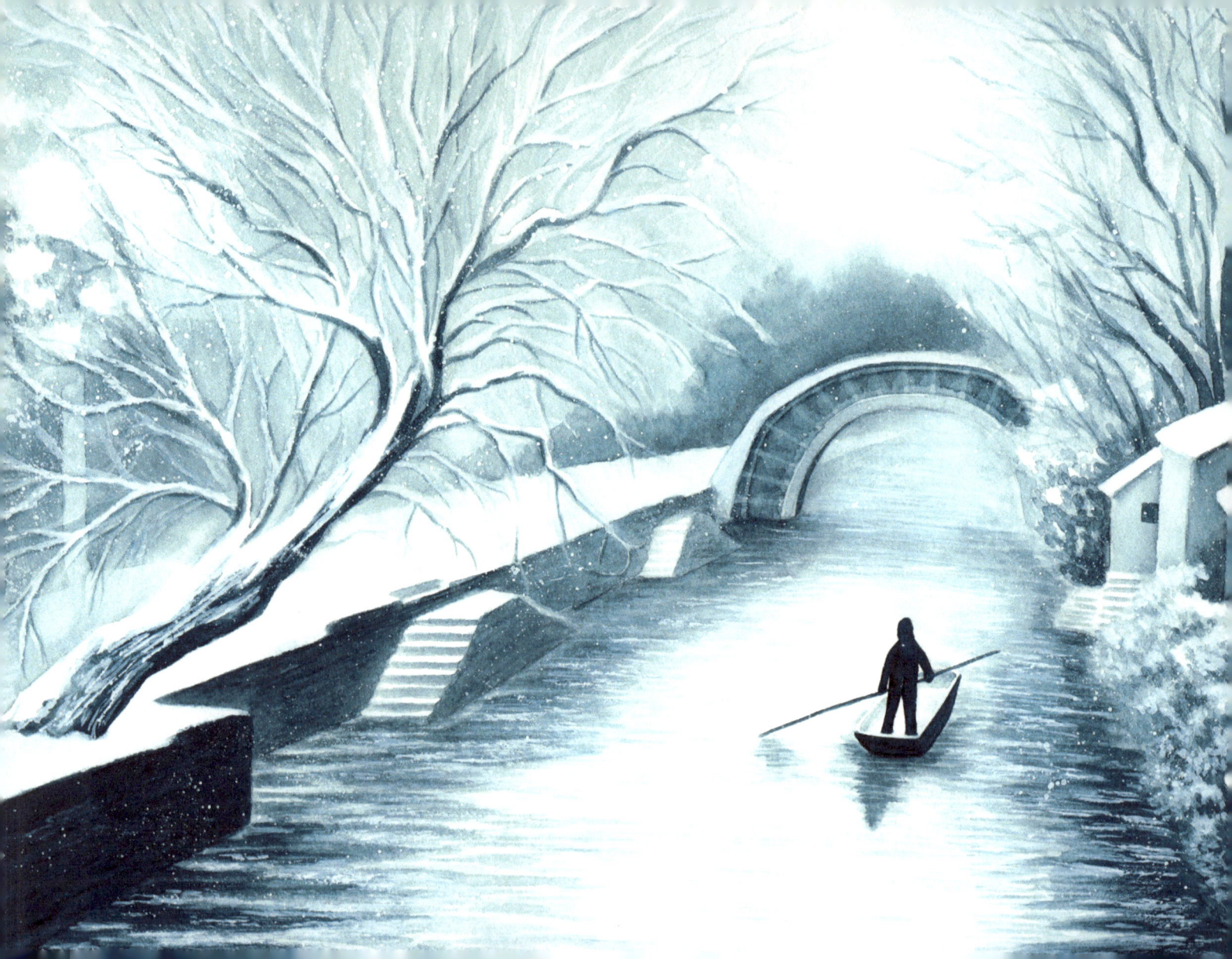

www.ingramcontent.com/pod-product-compliance
Lightning Source LLC
Chambersburg PA
CBHW050738180526
45159CB00003B/1276